Spiritual

Warrior

The Art of Spiritual Living

CRITICAL ACCLAIM
FOR SPIRITUAL WARRIOR

"*Spiritual Warrior* is a life-changing book. John-Roger echoes my own intense desire to preserve spiritual focus in a world filled with distraction and anxiety. I welcome his crystal-clear light on the pathway of self-discovery. I found the words of a wise, practical man in *Spiritual Warrior*."

John Bradshaw
Author of *Bradshaw On The Family, Creating Love, Homecoming*
Emmy-winning host of PBS TV specials, "Bradshaw On The Family,"
"Family Secrets"

"I have always loved reading of warriors, eagerly seeking the qualities that would enable me to overcome my life's obstacles. And, I have always sought for loving in my life, that eventually I found the most fulfilled in my love of God. *Spiritual Warrior* illumined for me how to put together the Spirit and the warrior in me in the most practical of ways. Now, I am learning that no matter the outer circumstances, I am the happiness and love and success that I was seeking."

Leigh Taylor-Young
Emmy-winning actress ("Picket Fences," "Sunset Beach")
Special Advisor in Arts/Media for the United Nations Environment Program
Spokesperson for the Institute for Individual and World Peace

"I loved *Spiritual Warrior*. John-Roger redefines dedication, commitment, cooperation, enthusiasm, and empathy. He encourages us to be heroic 'warriors of love' in our own lives, and to 'win' to the benefit of all—complete with material success and spiritual fulfillment. We learn to turn chaos into creativity, negative fantasy into divine imagination, to own the mantle of 'Spiritual Warrior' and to share it. It's brilliant!"

Sally Kirkland
Oscar nominee and Golden Globe-winning actress (*Anna*)
Producer, Director, Teacher

"It's rare that one book is both inspiring and practical. *Spiritual Warrior* not only inspires us each to step forward on the warrior's path armed with love, intention, forgiveness and simplicity, but also provides us with a manual for using them. Especially helpful is the fifteen-day spiritual convergence process which pushes the fledgling warrior out of the nest."

Drs. Ron and Mary Hulnick
Co-Directors of the University of Santa Monica

"*Spiritual Warrior* offers a wealth of experience and continuous references for conscious living from the Spirit. John-Roger gives us common sense tools for maintaining our inner focus in this challenging and sometimes disturbing world. As human beings, we all share in the collective search for meaning and a return to living in our true home, the Soul."

John Morton
Spiritual Director, Movement of Spiritual Inner Awareness
J-R's golf buddy

Books by John-Roger

Awakening Into Light
Baraka
Blessings of Light
Buddha Consciousness
The Christ Within & The Disciples of Christ with the Cosmic Christ Calendar
The Consciousness of Soul
A Consciousness of Wealth
Dream Voyages
Drugs
Dynamics of the Lower Self
Forgiveness: The Key to the Kingdom
God Is Your Partner
Inner Worlds of Meditation
The Journey of a Soul
Loving . . . Each Day
Manual on Using the Light
The Master Chohans of the Color Rays
Passage Into Spirit
The Path to Mastership
Possessions, Projections & Entities
The Power Within You
Psychic Protection
Q & A Journal from the Heart
Relationships: The Art of Making Life Work
Sex, Spirit & You
The Signs of the Times
The Sound Current
The Spiritual Family
The Spiritual Promise
Spiritual Warrior
The Tao of Spirit
Walking with the Lord
The Way Out Book
Wealth & Higher Consciousness

For Further Information, Please Contact:

MSIA®
P.O. Box 513935
Los Angeles, CA 90051-1935
213/737-4055
soul@msia.org
www.msia.org

Spiritual

Warrior

The Art of Spiritual Living

John-Roger

Mandeville Press
Los Angeles, California

Published by Mandeville Press
P.O. Box 513935
Los Angeles,California 90051-1935
e-mail: jrbooks@msia.org

Visit us on the Web at www.spiritualwarrior.org

Printed in the United States of America
ISBN 0-914829-36-X

Library of Congress Catalog Card Number: 97-75595

Passage from John Le Carré's *The Secret Pilgrim*
reprinted by permission of Knopf, Inc.

To Claire
From your Abba

CONTENTS

Part III: ADVANCED TRAINING

"I had found what I was looking for—a man like myself but one who in his search for meaning had discovered a worthwhile object for his life; who had paid every price and not counted it a sacrifice; who was paying it still and would pay it till he died; who cared nothing for compromise, nothing for his pride, nothing for ourselves or the opinion of others; who had reduced his life to the one thing that mattered to him, and was free."

—John Le Carré, *The Secret Pilgrim*

Author's Note

In writing about spiritual concepts, I will inevitably use words that mean different things to different people, depending upon either the personal path they have taken or their spiritual or religious upbringing. In the pages that follow, I have used words like "Soul," "soul," "Spirit," "spirit," "Self," "self," "God," and others, in specific ways. To get the most out of this book, I suggest readers suspend, as much as possible, their personal interpretations of these words and concepts and stay open to how I define them in context, by my explanations, and by their own intuitive sense.

Preface

I have learned what it means to be a Spiritual Warrior out of practical necessity. Over the past few years, my own work and personality have come under heavy criticism by some people who didn't agree with what I was doing. For me, the best response to this has been to live happily and successfully regardless of what has been said or done. I have endeavored to live my life internally, without attachment to the world. That is the way of the Spiritual Warrior.

This book is an attempt to share with you the principles of the process I have learned and to teach you how you can apply these principles in your own life, whatever your circumstances. I know they work, because I have tried and tested all these principles time and time again in my own life.

Since I am a practical man, this is a practical book. My approach is *not* like fine china that is taken out carefully and used once a year. There is no point in having a philosophy, no matter how beautiful or poetic, that can't be used every day.

Over the years I've read many books written about

the warrior approach to life, including excellent books by Carlos Castaneda, which have addressed certain aspects of the process. People still come to me, however, asking how they can live an inner spiritual life in a constantly changing, challenging, and demanding world.

This book is an answer to that question. As you read it, I urge you to use what works for you and let go of what doesn't. In fact, that principle, applied to your entire life, is the first step along the path of the Spiritual Warrior. Join me in taking it right now.

John-Roger
Los Angeles, 1997

Introduction: Why a Warrior?

This book will teach you how to claim the mantle of the Spiritual Warrior. Spiritual Warriors are people—men and women—who confidently make choices about where to focus their internal attention, even when the external realities of their everyday lives are chaotic, troublesome, or just plain annoying.

Although the word "warrior" may bring to mind images of armed conflict, becoming a Spiritual Warrior has nothing to do with violence. The positive attributes of a warrior—dedication, commitment, discipline, and focus—can also serve us on our personal spiritual paths.

A warrior's sense of mission is clear, and his attention is impeccably focused on his goal, even in the face of emotional crisis, illness, conflicts with a spouse, a co-worker, a neighbor, or the person who just cut him off on the freeway.

Even when confronted with adversity, the classic warrior holds fast to his values and principles. But while most warriors march off to subdue a perceived enemy, Spiritual Warriors

follow a different path, marching into their own innermost center. They strive to perfect the internal discipline that will keep them attuned to God (or Spirit, if you prefer that term) as they journey through this world.

Three qualities are especially vital to the Spiritual Warrior: Intention, impeccability, and ruthlessness.

Intention is the direction we want to travel. Spiritual Warriors make sure their intention is very clear because what we put out into the world is what we get back. If your intention is to be loving and caring, you cannot let anything that is not loving or caring come into your field of action.

Impeccability is, quite simply, using our energy wisely and purposefully, conserving and directing it so that we align ourselves with Spirit. From this spiritual alignment emerges clarity about eternal reality and freedom from the binding nature of the physical world.

Ruthlessness is the Spiritual Warrior's Sword of Truth, the Sword of the Heart, which cuts away all that is no longer necessary or useful. Spiritual Warriors do not accept just anything and everything but are ruthless about ridding themselves of limitations and addictions—the habitual unproductive behaviors of the past.

The Purpose of Becoming a Spiritual Warrior

Spiritual Warriors are open to the world, not shut off from it. They do not ask to control it but accept it as it is and seek inner guidance in order to respond to it in ways that are aligned with their highest intentions. They know that the fears, aggravations, and confusions of life aren't accidental; instead, our Souls can take advantage of the particular opportunities they offer—opportunities to learn, grow, and share.

Life is not a matter of avoiding the tough lessons, but of extracting all we can from them for the advancement of our spiritual selves. The difference between a Spiritual Warrior and a lot of other people who wander around waiting for success, or love, or abundance to happen to them is that the Spiritual Warrior *acts*, not reacts.

The Five Characteristics of the Spiritual Warrior

As long as we are hampered by our old mindsets, even formulating our highest intention will be a daunting task. Take this example. If we want to make more money, but believe that the kind of work we do can only pay what we are currently making, we have already made it impossible to achieve our goal. We need constantly to shake up the old and make room for the new. More importantly, we need to practice being in Spirit, being in alignment with our spiritual intention, so that it becomes our habitual state. This book will not waste your time by attempting to change your behavior or rid you of your negative patterns. Such attempts are invariably futile. You won't find any easy way to lose weight, quit smoking, or make a million dollars in these pages.

However, change will take place naturally as you adopt the simple principles and tools offered here.

Ultimately, we are going to upgrade our addictions—our habits, the things that trap us—to God. So what we want now is to orient our addictive patterns toward God, so that we keep moving toward our intention.

Incorporating these five characteristics into everything you do will bring you closer to your inner Spirit each day:

1. **The Spiritual Warrior accepts all things.** This means no judgment and no resistance. (No one ever said that these practices were easy!)

2. **The Spiritual Warrior cooperates with all things.** You know you are not in control, but it looks as if you are.

3. **The Spiritual Warrior understands all things.** This doesn't mean you can explain everything that is going on within you; you just have to awaken to your experience of it. Then understanding appears.

4. **The Spiritual Warrior has enthusiasm for all things.** When you open to the Spirit, Its energy pours through you, and you regain the wonder and awe of life.

5. **The Spiritual Warrior has empathy for all things.** Others are going through the same trials as you, so there is no need to feel superior or inferior.

The Plan of This Book

When we incorporate these characteristics into everything we do, they steer us toward our intention. But the task of developing these characteristics and becoming a Spiritual Warrior is formidable. The goal of *Part* I of this book is to help you wake yourself up spiritually, identify and clear away your "internal adversaries" like addictive behaviors, and equip you with your "spiritual weaponry." Think of it as boot camp for the Spiritual Warrior. *Part* II intensifies your training as you develop the more difficult skills of the Spiritual Warrior. Finally, the *Fifteen-Day Journal* that concludes the book represents a kind of advanced training that will allow you to put into practice the principles you've learned.

As you begin your training in Spiritual Warriorhood, remember that its purpose is to affirm and strengthen the best inside you and to support you in reaping the abundance that this world can offer. Also remember that what you may desire right now will probably not be what you desire once you realize your inner self, your True Self. But that is for you to discover as you undertake this journey. The mantle of the Spiritual Warrior is attainable by everyone, but it requires a different way of proceeding through life, one which will be challenging. Those who do practice the art of the Spiritual Warrior will find that the rewards are tremendous.

PART I

RECLAIMING YOUR
INNER TERRITORY

Chapter 1

Surrendering Control

At the root of our emotional addictions
is our belief structure,
which continually undermines us
by telling us two things:
(1) that we will be alone or abandoned, and
(2) that we will lose control of reality.

Many people have asked me, "By what authority do you speak?" After all, I am not a rabbi, a priest, or anyone "official." Yet I could ask, "By what authority do you question?" The "authority" to question and to speak out are both inherent within each one of us. I say what I say because I can.

Many people never do speak out because they don't trust themselves or are afraid of the reactions of others. When we are not aligned with our Soul, we need the outside world to validate our religious or spiritual positions. We want something "official" to tell us we are on the right track. If we suffer, more often than not we think it is a punishment, something "God has done to me." This is a form of spiritual immaturity, and it holds us back from our best selves.

As we become spiritually mature, we attune to our Soul nature. We participate. We see that the world is the screen upon which we project ourselves, so if we see flaws out there, we are the ones who need to change. And this change can only take place by discovering our true nature, the Divine within us.

You are the first cause, and you are the first effect. You are the last cause and the last effect. So, inside of you is the only place that change can be made. You can indulge the illusion of changing things in the world, but unless you change them in yourself, no true change has taken place.

The deck may have been shuffled and the cards may be in a different order, but it is the same deck with the same patterns. If we want to attune to our spiritual selves and, in doing so, reap the rewards of the outside world, the Soul must be taken back into God and become a co-creator. The first step in reclaiming our inner territory—so that we may ultimately become co-creators and Spiritual Warriors—is to confront the habitual practices, or "addictions," that stand in our way.

Everyday Addictions

Like it or not, you interpret life according to your belief system. Even though you may think your beliefs are better than others'—more accepting, more open—they are still beliefs. If I put water in a glass, then pour it into a cup, what is the difference in the water? Obviously, none. The water is what it always is; it has just been put in different containers. In the same way the Divine has always been the Divine. But humans have denied this by playing the game of alienation and separation; and they have played the game so well that they have gotten caught in it.

One way we stay caught is through our addictive behaviors. When our habits become so entrenched that we can't get out of them, they are, for all intents and purposes, addictions. The neural system picks up patterns very easily. In a flash we can train ourselves to need cigarettes or alcohol, to love chocolate; we develop addictions and dependencies of all kinds, physical and emotional. It is so easy, it is amazing; it is frightening.

Just take a look at your everyday addictions to see how true this is. If the first thing you do in the morning is

John-Roger

swing your feet onto the floor, then put on your slippers, first the left and then the right, *stop*. Next time, put your right slipper on, then your left; and not only that, swing off the other side of the bed. When you start interrupting your patterns, you'll be shocked at how odd it feels, and you will think, "I'm really out of sync with myself today." Why? Because you are breaking out of the mold, you are out of the rut, and you are refocusing.

But physical habits are easy to change in comparison to emotional addictions. One bad affair, one bad relationship, may make you single for life. At the root of our emotional addictions is our belief structure, which continually undermines us by telling us two things: (1) that we will be alone or abandoned, and (2) that we will lose control of reality.

Control as the Master Addiction

The fear of losing control is the strongest human motivator. Control is the master addiction. It is not lack of courage that keeps us from moving forward, as most people think; it is the fear of losing control. We want to control, and when we feel we can't, we freeze; we stop. The person who fears loss of control is like a deer caught in the headlights: Instead of running off the highway to safety, it stops in its tracks.

To some extent we are all control freaks. We want to control events, so that we can always be certain of the outcome. We put pressure on ourselves to master the events of our lives. But this does not give us control; it just gives us pressure.

What you are really saying in this struggle for control

is, "I'm fearful that I won't succeed." In a very subtle way, that fear is a form of atheism because it tells you, "There's no God to help you." You move into doubt, and you freeze again.

When we doubt, we are saying, "I don't know." And our fear whispers to us, "It is unknowable... you are out of control."

Spiritual Warriors turn doubt into a tool. They don't attempt to control it, but they refuse to let it control them. They use it the same way you use a guard rail when you are on a highway running alongside a steep cliff: To mark the boundary between the road and the void. As soon as you feel doubt, move back in until you find yourself once more on firm ground.

Making a Friend of Fear

We humans are complex, multifaceted beings. When we are afraid, our fear dominates everything else. It brings us to a halt.

But that's because we won't sit still with fear. We won't be patient. We won't come to this moment and simply be present in reality. We latch on to a relationship, an idea, a symbol, anything to distract us from our fear and avoid coming into friendship with its energy.

But we have so badly mislabeled this fear. It is not just fear; it is also an expression of the Divine—as indeed everything is an expression of the Divine. The Divine is so powerful that if it were served to us in the way we want it—neatly arranged on a platter in bite-sized, easy-to-digest portions—we would not recognize it. So it comes in like a typhoon, like a tidal wave. We say, "Oh my God!" And that is exactly what it is.

But if you realize that the tidal wave is just allegorical and cannot harm you, then you are able to stand in it and do nothing. It envelopes you and you realize that you are in the Divine. (And all that time you were afraid of it.)

The experience is like that of the fellow who won't ask a particular girl to dance because he is afraid she will reject him. Meanwhile, she is waiting, indeed hoping, to be asked; that's why she's there. Yet for him the fear of rejection overrides the desire for the dance. In the same way, the Divine is waiting to be asked, and we don't ask it because we also are afraid of rejection, of losing control, of being abandoned, of being lonely.

Get friendly with fear. When it comes along, say, "Come and sit down, my friend; let's see what you've got going." Sit with it. Observe it. Say, "This is fear; this is my friend."

Most of us consider fear to be an enemy. How can it be your friend? Because it is going to reveal its great power—the knowledge that it is merely a veil which conceals the Divine from us. We have kept ourselves from seeing and knowing the power because it comes disguised as fear. If someone came up to you and said, "I'm going to reveal to you the great power of the universe," would you look at them as an enemy?

Surrendering Control

Once we understand that we cannot have control, then we can surrender to what is in control; God, and let Him continue to run the universe. Sometimes we sense God's hidden power, but we feel it as fear and we contract. But there is nothing in God to inspire fear: Fear is only the label we put on our own awe, and perhaps bewilderment, when we sense His power, a power we cannot possibly comprehend, and we fear we are losing control.

We all want to experience living and vitality. We also want life very safe and secure and under our control. But anyone who ever feared doing something, and then went ahead and did it, embraced the enemy. And the fear turned into confidence and a great sense of accomplishment. These people will be eager to do the same thing again. The first time may have been an accident, or luck, but the second time will be a determined choice. And once we make a determined choice to do something, we become free in it. Not free *from* it, but free *in* it.

Perfect Surrender Is Perfect Protection

We often need to surrender control in order to receive whatever it is we are asking for. Most people look at surrender as a negative; they think it means defeat. But look at it this way: To surrender is to protect yourself from further harm or hurt. Every country that surrenders immediately starts healing and building. Every country that keeps fighting an impossible battle and won't surrender keeps going downhill, killing, and destroying itself. When I was younger, the cry was "Uncle." You would fight a person, get him down and hold him. When he would say, "Uncle," you would let him up, and the fight would be over. To surrender is to stop fighting. It is not cowardice. It is often the wisest choice.

Belief Structure Versus Reality

We must continue maturing. It is our nature to grow, to expand. And when we are not growing and expanding, we have aches and pains, suffering and anguish, because our nature pushes against us, demanding growth. We are afraid to change; we struggle mightily to stay at a familiar level, to remain as we have always been. But that is a lie. Life simply doesn't work that way.

Now that you know that control is the master addiction, and you are prepared to surrender control, and to feel the fear and go with it, you know one of the greatest secrets of the Spiritual Warrior: *Expand in the midst of contraction*.

Secret of the Spiritual Warrior: Expand in the Midst of Contraction

Negative thinking, playing the victim, holding on to hurts, complaining—All are contracted states. They move us away from awareness.

The number one enemy of the Spiritual Warrior is resistance. Resistance is the ultimate contracted state; it produces discord, disease, and violence. When we resist our own divine nature, we commit an act of violence against ourselves. Ironically, when we resist our *dark* nature it is also an act of violence. For people seeking a path of awareness, resistance can become either a stepping-stone or a stumbling block.

But you can't overcome resistance by resisting it.

The Spiritual Warrior lives life spontaneously, constantly letting go. The ordinary person wants to justify things. They want recognition for what they accomplish, and they want to blame someone for what doesn't go right. If they can't find a reason, they will make a reason, and that reason, in their minds, will always be perfect. If that reason is refuted, they will find another to take its place.

So here's the key: *Forget your reasons; they will*

always be perfect. They don't mean anything. Reasons keep us in a contracted state. You do not need to justify your life. Just live. Be spontaneous and do what your heart prompts you to do. You do not have to wait for numerous things to fall into place in order to relax. Just relax. Someone doesn't have to make you laugh. Just laugh. How simple that is, and yet we won't do it . . . because we have all the reasons not to.

Ultimately, the way to expand is simply to let go of resistance.

Chapter 2

Accepting the Enemy Within

We have to go into the dark part of ourselves

and love that dark part.

For loving it is the key to the Kingdom.

And we have to stand up

and acknowledge

that it is part of us.

As Spiritual Warriors we must not become victims, no matter what is happening. That does not mean that we can't say "stop." But we shouldn't say it as victims. Alternately, as we move through life and try to accomplish things, we often bump into other people—a spouse, a boss, a child, a relative, a neighbor—and discover that even though we have been trying to conduct ourselves honorably, others perceive themselves as the victims of our actions. The Spiritual Warrior banishes all traces of victimhood.

Victimhood means letting your emotions dictate your consciousness. How does that happen? There is a dark side within us, and we must learn to confront it. That dark side is an enemy to all our highest intentions. It is like the little devil in the cartoon that sits on our shoulder and whispers to us. It tells us all the negative things about the world, about other people. It tells us how bad they really are. It tells us the terrible things they do.

The Unconscious

According to classic psychology, when you tell others about the terrible things that they do, you are projecting. I see evidence of it every day. For example, I receive letters from people around the world telling me what terrible things have been done to them by others, things which have wounded them and hampered them in their spiritual growth. But, often enough, when I investigate the situation on my own, I find that their claims of being victims have little or no validity.

So where did these vivid impressions of mistreatment and cruelty come from? They came from inside the person who complained. He or she was full of repressed feelings of resentment and injury which had become totally centered on another person. To victims it always seems that the emotions they have projected on their enemy are radiating from the enemy. Projection is demonizing, dehumanizing. If we declare another person to be essentially wrong, bad, evil, then we feel that whatever we do to them, they deserve.

If we are going to do anything on the planet worthwhile for ourselves or anyone else, we have to watch out primarily for these insidious mindsets that sabotage all our good works: The victim and the enemy within. You are the one who makes yourself the victim. And who is the enemy? It's you. You are the enemy and the victim at one and the same time!

One of the finest stories I know is that of the Prodigal Son. In this parable, the younger of two sons asks his father for his inheritance. Having received it, he goes off to a distant country where he squanders the whole of his fortune in drunkenness and carousing. Finding himself at length utterly destitute, he resolves to return home and throw himself on the mercy of his father.

His father receives him with open arms. But the older brother, who has been working hard all these years, loving and serving his father, is not particularly happy about his brother's return. He sulks and considers the honor lavished on his prodigal brother as a tacit affront to himself.

By putting this story into a psychological framework, we can gain greater understanding of this process of projection. There's a part of you that goes out and has fun and dances and carouses and loses all your money. And there's another part of you that is righteous, steadfast, does all the work, obeys all the rules. These are two parts of the same personality. The righteous part, the older brother, says, "I don't want this renegade back in our house." But the Soul, the mediator of our personality says, "Wait a minute, that part belongs here, just as you do. This is his home just as it is yours." So you grudgingly allow it to stay. Then, when you see someone do something that *resembles* what your dark side has done, you project your judgement of your dark side onto the other person—and they may not be doing what you think they are doing.

In order to be more clear, more in control of yourself, you cannot reject your dark side: You must embrace it as your brother, as the other part of your personality. In the Christian Bible it says, "Let God make perfect in you what was started." What does that "perfect" mean? Is it some sort of utopian ideal? Does it mean that your feet don't get dirty, that you walk on water, you float through the air? The word "perfect" from the Aramaic means "brought to completion." The perfected state is not an elevated state, but a completed one.

The first of the five characteristics of the Spiritual Warrior is *acceptance*. If you look into some part of you and say, "That part has inappropriate thoughts. That part desires to do inappropriate things. That part tells me lies. If people knew what I thought and what I desired, they'd never talk to me again. I'm terrible!"—what does that say about your levels of acceptance? Spiritual Warriors don't chafe against the limitations of human nature. They no longer struggle to be free of their darker side, and when acceptance occurs, the shackles that bound us to it seem to vanish.

Our Own Worst Enemy

Good men and women live on this planet. Yet we look strangely at someone who says, "I'm a good person." We would be much more comfortable hearing, "I'm a sinful, bad person." I have difficulty understanding this thinking. Why can't a person own up to his or her goodness? Why is it unusual to own up to how good you are, how spiritual you are, and how beautiful you are? Why would you readily confess to being a creep, to wasting your life, to being full of guilt and anxiety?

The Spiritual Warrior has no time for false modesty and low self esteem. Understand right now that you may not be worthy of God, but you are worthwhile to God. Without knowing you, I can assure you you are worthwhile! No matter how sinful or ignorant people are, they are worthwhile.

If you refuse to accept your own worth, your own goodness, and your own abilities, the way of the Spiritual Warrior is not for you. It is so important to have a good (a God) point of view about yourself or you can never arrive at higher consciousness. You will only arrive at feelings of unworthiness and worthlessness. And when you declare yourself to be worthless, you are denying God's love for you; you aren't even giving Him a chance to love you.

Your destiny, what you are here to learn and what you are here to do, is sitting inside of you. So is the dark side; so is the enemy. How hard it is to accept this, that the light and the dark can and *must* co-exist within us!

In the Christian Bible it is written, "Seek first the Kingdom of Heaven and all the rest will be added unto you." What does that mean to people? That you must have the Kingdom of Heaven first and then all the rest will be given to you. But read the passage again. It does not say that at all. It says *seek*, not *have*.

Tapping Our Creativity

As we seek, what do we discover in this "Kingdom of Heaven"? Few people know it, but it is creativity. And where does the energy for it come from? Out of the great cesspool of the unconscious.

When we tap the unconscious—and this can be triggered any number of ways, through smell, movement, color—energy is released. Our ego tries to suppress this energy, fearing the newness, the freedom it offers. But if we don't open up the unconscious and let its contents out, at some point it comes bursting out on its own, at its worst in the form of a psychological deviation or physical illness.

But properly tapped, the unconscious is a repository of wealth. We have to go into the dark part of ourselves and love that dark part. For loving it is the key to the Kingdom. And we have to stand up and acknowledge that it is part of us.

I have often heard people say, "Once I confessed my ignorance and accepted the unknowable darkness in myself, I felt wonderfully freed." Of course they feel free, because they are no longer suppressing that great energy, and shutting off the Spirit; instead they are thriving on it. They are no longer saying, "I reject that; it is not, cannot, be a part of me." Instead they say, "This is truly what I am, where I am at this moment."

Children are for me like windows into the immense energy of the unconscious. There is a little girl in my life, Claire. Guess what Claire does with me? Anything she wants. She is so totally at ease, so free with me, it can be astonishing. If I resisted her, treating her like an adult or an opponent, wanting to change her, to improve her, not only would I be absurd, I would lose all her brightness, her beauty and wonder. To deny her would be tantamount to denying God. However, to acknowlege her closeness to God is not to say that she doesn't get dirty while playing.

Children can teach us so much if we have the wit to understand that they are teachers. Inside Claire is the great unconscious. She has tapped into it automatically; she knows it, draws her energy from it, and has her independence in it. She is at once a little angel and a little tyrant and she gets what she wants. I could easily play the victim when she interrupts me, but that would be denying all the goodness and beauty she brings.

And why not receive everyone as I receive her? Why play the victim with anyone, young or old? It's not that you have to participate with everyone you meet. You choose to what degree you want to become involved. But if we do not acknowledge our irritation or joy, and so master it, it will drive us crazy. We will get nervous, irritable, upset. We will have attacks of terror, anxiety, or depression. All these feelings are nothing but signs that we are not acknowledging parts of ourselves.

You may be thinking, "But you don't know what I've been through, what a struggle, what a battle my life has been!" I understand that, but remember that everyone has struggled. It's not the trouble and pain you've been through that makes you special. In every situation, we have only one option: To embrace it anyway. Sit down when things are going badly, even when all hell is breaking loose, and say, "I love me anyway."

Saying it one time is not enough. You may still be as vulnerable as you were before. So once you start, just keep moving forward without looking back. If you look back, you will only see that you are in unfamiliar territory, and your fear will say, "You don't know what's going on, you don't know where you're going, you don't know how you got here."

A last word on victims and enemies.

What I present outwardly is not my true self. You see me by reflected light. But I am Light, not reflected light. So are you.

So I never take you at face value, but I accept you both in your essence and in the way you present yourself to me.

Loving Your Enemy Inside

Can you face an enemy and say, "I love you?" Especially a stubborn enemy inside you? Yes, you can, and I will tell you what happens when you do. Once you truly embrace the dark side, it turns to help you. Then you don't have stubbornness, you have determination. The darkness transformed the moment you accepted it, and all the power that was blocking you before now becomes the power of ascension, of upliftment.

When you feel really negative and you talk about it—not as a victim but as a way of facing the enemy and loving it—you are saying, "Out of God come all things." All things. That includes the negative things, too. Negative doesn't mean bad; we make things bad by judging them.

Critical Thinking

One day a fellow asked me, "Is this just positive thinking?" I said, "What do you mean, *just*?" But no, it is not the same. If you practice positive thinking, you'll feel you've failed when you find yourself in negative thinking. And this can be very discouraging, especially if you are anything like me, with a tremendous talent for thinking negative thoughts.

I prefer to practice critical thinking. I don't mean "critical" in the sense of "criticizing." Critical thinking is the process of examining the possibilities, looking at potential outcomes. It becomes negative only if I project my emotion on it. But if I can employ my intellect, just observing, looking, sorting, I can turn the possibilities into usable commodities.

How does it work? Here is a little metaphor. You go into a dark room, looking for something. You're not sure where exactly it is in the room. Rather than groping around in the dark for it, the critical thinker looks first for the light switch. When the room is flooded with light it is an easy matter to find what you are looking for.

Practicing Positive Focus

Since the direction of this critical thinking is positive, yet it's not positive thinking, what is it? It is positive focus. Why positive focus, rather than positive thinking? With positive thinking, we can be drowning but telling ourselves that things are just great. With positive focus we tell ourselves things will be great—as soon as we get to shore. Then we focus on the shore and get moving. We say, "I am moving toward a goal. I see it. If negative thoughts arise, they will not stop me from getting there because I can still see my goal. I can maneuver around the negativity and remain headed in my positive direction. I may even tap into the enemy for my uplift. I may befriend it and convert it to my own use."

How can something negative push you back in line? Let's say you are doing important work and the phone rings. You forgot to turn on the answering machine and the person calling knows you are there. You can either get frustrated and irritated and answer in a huff, or you can use the phone ringing to remind you to take a breath, to stretch, to say a quick prayer for your children.

Becoming Whole

I am convinced that all of the negative things we hear or do, or that other people do, boil down to two primary motivations: I want to give love and I want to receive love. Then why not, right this moment, steel ourselves against failure, against subterfuge, against deception, and cut straight to love?

We cannot go anywhere in the Spirit world without taking our beingness with us. It is our entirety, which means that it includes all facets of the personality and the Soul. When we start to become whole and complete, the goodness of God in us starts to flow up and out, and takes the personality and lifts it up. That doesn't mean that the negative side won't still nag away at us. But if we acknowledge the negative side, it will lose its power and will cease to control us.

Have you ever done something and then said, "What a waste?" Of course you have. But with a positive focus, you can say, "It was not a waste. That time I was wrong, next time I will be free to do it right." But if you defend your mistake, putting forth reasons and excuses, you cannot advance in life; you have nailed yourself to your mistake.

When baby elephants are trained, the trainers take a large chain and wrap it around the elephant's leg and then tie it to a big stake that is anchored deep in the ground. And they let the baby elephant pull and pull until it realizes it can't go anywhere. They do this for two or three years and then they take a small stake and pound it into the ground and tether the elephant to it with a rope. The elephant judges by its own experience and never even tries to budge it. A huge animal becomes victim to a flimsy piece of rope, and it is as firmly held by that as if it were bound with iron chains.

When we play the victim we are behaving like this elephant. We act human, we talk human, but we respond like an animal. Yet all it takes is one fresh look, one totally new thought, to free us completely.

Once you love the enemy inside, once you embrace it, that enemy will transform and yield its power to you. At that moment, you are sitting on the most wonderful wealth of your existence. The ability to do, the strength to do it, and the energy to complete it; that is the true wealth. Out of that come our health and our happiness.

Tool of the Spiritual Warrior: Clearing the Unconscious with Free-Form Writing

The unconscious is one of our most powerful influences because by its very nature we cannot be aware of its influence until it surfaces. We may find ourselves thinking, feeling, and doing things that we can't explain, or experiencing illness or pain with an unknown cause. The vastness of the unconscious is impossible to explore. It marks the division between our waking awareness and our true spiritual nature. To become aware of our Soul we have to cross that line into the unconscious. As we do so, we lose something of our daylight awareness. That is why so many people talk about their spiritual nature but so few are aware of it as a living experience.

The chief intention of Spiritual Warriors is to become aware of their spiritual nature. I have stated my own intention this way: "I'm keeping my eyes on You, Lord, only You." You may want to put this intention into different words, but the basic idea will be the same for us all.

For years, I have used free-form writing to help clear my unconscious. It is very simple to do. I have described below the way I approach it; you can modify these suggestions to suit your own needs.

1. *Find a quiet place and sit down with a ballpoint pen and paper.*

I recommend you light a candle. Sometimes as you write, emotional negativity will come up and release into the room. Since it tends to go toward flame, this may keep the room clear and the negativity away from you.

One thing you do not do in this process is let the pen write and then read what it has written. That is automatic writing, a very different process.

2. *Allow a thought into your mind and transfer it into the pen.*

You may not even finish a sentence before the next thought comes up. For example, the thought, "go to the restaurant together" arises. As you start to write "together" you may get T-O-G-E . . . and then the next word or thought that comes up is "help" and you may write H-L-P. That is just fine because you know what you mean by it.

It is important that you do not do free-form writing on a computer or a typewriter. Free-form writing is a kinesthetic activity: The neural impulses from the fingers are sent back to the brain so that the writing actually releases and records the patterns of the unconscious. I call them the "beach balls," those things we have suppressed for a long, long, time and have expended energy to keep under the surface. They can carry tremendous emotion. So at times you may end up writing very forcefully. That's why I recommend that you do not write with a pencil: The lead can break and you lose the flow.

In some instances you will find yourself writing as fast as you can, and at other times you will be writing slowly. But throughout this process you should be writing continuously because there are always thoughts in your mind—and you are to write them down, even if they are, "Gee, I don't know why I'm doing this. What should I write next? HMMMM."

3. *When you get through writing, do not read it over. Rip up what you have written and burn it.*

After you have done free-form writing for any length of time you will start to get some beautiful, inspirational, wonderful prose which you will want to keep. And when you are through with your session you will forget where the beautiful writing was and will want to read through what you wrote to find it. Do not do this because the energy and negativity that you released onto the paper can return to you if you reread it. Instead, as you are writing, and thoughts are flowing through, take the pieces of paper on which you write the inspirational thoughts and set them aside, separate from the other writing. When you finish your session, rewrite the sections you want to keep in a special book. Then you can rip up and burn all the original pages.

4. *Be aware that you are not giving yourself over to anything in this process because you are in absolute control of what is happening.*

As you do this, a wonderful thing can take place. Because your writing is often a symbol of an inner disturbance, you may find that pressure leaves you as you write. Obsessive behavior, habitual patterns suddenly disappear, and you won't even know what it was that was inside you or how it managed to get there. You will just know that it is gone. Often it will feel like relief or a sense that somebody has taken a weight off you. The strange thing is that you will probably not be aware that it was there until it is gone! Such is the nature of the unconscious.

When it goes, I would strongly advise you not even to question what it was, because you might find it and re-establish it inside. We are powerful creators. Just by thinking about how glad you are to be rid of it you could reactivate your own memory of it and—poof!—it's in.

I emphasize this because it is very hard to get something out a second time. I am speaking from personal experience. I re-looked at something, and it took me fifteen years before I was able to clear it again. I was aware every day that I had not cleared it, so I just kept at it. And one day it went. I knew what it was when it released because of where it was expressing in my body. And I just smiled and got busy doing something else to distract my mind so I would not go back to see if I had really released it. There is something crazy about our human minds. We say, "But is it really gone?" And, in doing so, we bring it back. It's as if we were to quit smoking, and then smoke another cigarette just to see if we really quit. Then we're hooked again. My advice is that when you let anything go, don't be concerned about it. Just let it go.

5. *Never share what you write with anyone else.*

If necessary, lock your door. If someone knocks, do not feel obligated to answer. You can tell people, "If my door is locked and it says, 'Do not disturb,' stay away. I will probably be out in a couple hours."

6. *Start slowly but work up to writing for at least an hour.*

Two hours per session is optimal. Each person is different, but to notice some real changes I recommend a minimum of three times a week for a minimum of three months. With practice you can get to the point where you can do this in fifteen minutes, but it will probably take you a year or so to get to that point.

The first time people approach this they usually sit down and think, "I wonder what I should write?" Instead, they should be writing, "I wonder what I should write? "Gee, this sure is stupid." "I think this makes me look like a fool." "I feel like such a phony." "Run . . . can't . . . yes . . . the elephant was there . . . no . . . the cows jumped . . . I can't . . . I don't know why I'm doing it." On to the next page.

You will see a flow begin, then all of a sudden it may become jumbled. You may think, "I wonder why I wrote 'green elephant?'" Don't start doing that. Instead, *write*, "I wonder why I wrote green elephant?" The writing will open the mind again and the repository of jumbled information that has been holding energy will start to release.

The Effects of Free-Form Writing

I have seen some phenomenal things occur with free-form writing; it has released people from psychologically restrictive patterns and from physical and emotional pain. Free-form writing does not do a great deal for you spiritually, but if you are feeling clearer and better about yourself there is a very good chance you will feel better about doing spiritual exercises, which *will* do things for you spiritually. (I will talk more about spiritual exercises later.) With your unconscious free, you will be in a better position to be aware of your Spirit.

As a stepping-stone to Soul awareness, free-form writing is wonderful. When I see people grieving over the death of their loved ones, I can get drawn into it in negative ways. So I will spend a lot of time writing to free myself from this restriction. You can have a tremendous amount of empathy for others without letting their grief drag you under.

Doodling is not the same as free-form writing. This process has to have some form. People ask if the color of the paper matters. The answer is: Only if you think so. Does the kind of ink matter? Only if you think so. One woman I know wrote with her finger and she got results. She would be sitting in meetings and would get mad about what people were doing. Right there she would write how mad she was on her hand with her finger. At the end of the meeting, she was no longer angry.

Free-form writing is like taking a onion and cutting a wedge through to the center. Then you leave a space, and cut another wedge, and so on. If you leave the onion exposed to the air after cutting several wedges and do no more, the sections of onion that were between the wedges will dry up and peel away. And after a time there will be just a tiny seed left. In the same way, by releasing some disturbances through free-form writing, others still inside of you will fall away.

When, after free-form writing, you realize that you have been carrying excessive weight or baggage, rejoice in the feeling of freedom. When something releases, immediately stand up, stretch, move around physically to experience your new freedom. If you let the area get rigid and tense, you may have another problem to deal with.

You will often feel a sense of diminishment taking place as though you are moving backwards inside of yourself, away from things; they are getting smaller and smaller as you move back. Don't be disturbed. That just means that you are moving away from the materiality of the world.

Free-form writing is a valuable tool of the Spiritual Warrior.

Chapter 3

Waking Yourself Up

When we observe,
we suddenly reach a state of peace,
which allows the Soul energy to activate.
When it activates, we attune to it.
We take hold of it
and we start riding back on this Soul energy
into our center.
We actually get beyond time.

Reclaiming our inner territory—the route to becoming a Spiritual Warrior—means learning to wake ourselves up. When we are attempting to wake up, we find ourselves involved in a process called unfolding. Many things will surface, and we will become aware that they have been taking up space in our inner territory. Many people find themselves resisting what surfaces, but that is futile. To reclaim our inner territory successfully—to maintain harmony and balance—is to enter a state of *observation*. This is often called "detachment," although that does not quite describe it. This chapter suggests ways of moving into this state. As you become more adept, you will realize that observation is one of the most valuable tools of the Spiritual Warrior.

Leaving It Alone

Often, as you begin to reclaim your inner territory, you find your mind running in many directions, full of thoughts, memories, ideas—good and bad, serious and trivial; and you wonder what to do in the face of all this commotion. The answer is, simply observe it. It is the same with what upsets you. When something annoying or upsetting presents itself to you, just stand back and say, "Here comes all that upset. How very interesting." Don't feel you have to put a lot of emotion into it, or fantasize about it.

As a Spiritual Warrior, you must realize that there is no substance to such emotions and fantasies. Instead of indulging the past, and making yourself a slave to it, through observation you will confront the upset and guilt of the past and stop it here and now. Most people think that when these thoughts occur to them, they have to *do* something about them: They have to explain, justify, feel guilt. But there is nothing you have to do except *observe*.

Here is a story. A little girl said to her father, "Daddy, there's a great big spider on the wall in my bedroom." And he said, "There is?" She said, "Well, I don't know if it's really on the wall or if it's just in my imagination." He said, "Well, go back in your bedroom and get in bed and just watch the spider." So she went back to bed and watched the spider on the wall and finally fell sleep. And the spider disappeared. It handled itself.

That is how it is with most things inside of us. Many people think they have to jump out of bed and get a shoe and smash the spider, when all they really have to do is observe it, let it disappear in its own time. In other words, leave it alone.

You can carry this principle into your everyday life. If you are having a problem with your children, just observe what they are doing. Reacting out of the emotions of the moment, imposing your own prejudiced concepts of how a child *should* behave, will only worsen the situation. Observe. Have patience.

You may ask, "What about planning ahead?" It's okay to *plan* ahead, but don't *emotionalize* ahead. You can use your imagination without projecting emotions into the future: Without fretting, worrying, anticipating troubles, and thereby actually creating troubles for yourself.

It is so easy to make ourselves sick by continuing to focus on our negativity, our judgments, our guilt, and our upset. So when those feelings appear, observe them. When a distraction appears, observe it. When your hand comes up in front of your face, observe it. If a fly buzzes around and is coming at you, observe it. But instead, many people cry, "Oh my God, here comes a fly, it is carrying disease!" Then they are off and running.

Impatience

We are such experts about what upsets us that it can go on without our even being aware of it, until one day we realize that we are feeling this enormous resentment and impatience within ourselves. When people come to me and tell me they have a lot of doubt, I usually find that they are just impatient. Often they don't have doubt, because they don't even know enough yet to doubt. If they don't know what is going on in the universe—and they usually don't—how can they possibly doubt it? They are just impatient for peace, for satisfaction. It is part of the human condition.

Impatience is part of our negativity, distracting us from our here-and-now life. So, what do you do with your impatience? You don't do anything with it, because impatience is doing something to you. All you have to do is observe it.

If there is food on the table and you have eaten enough, stop. Observe yourself. Watch what you are doing. If you have a headache and it feels like the worst headache in history, observe your headache. Close your eyes and *look* at it. You may say, "But every time I close my eyes, I think about it more and it hurts more." Yes, you think about it more. But thinking about it is not the same as observing it. Thinking can be a headache in itself! We learn nothing by fretting and becoming impatient. We don't grow. As Spiritual Warriors we want growth and expansion. So we observe.

When we observe, we suddenly reach a state of peace, which allows the Soul energy to activate. When it activates, we attune to it. We take hold of it and we start riding back on this Soul energy into our center. We actually get beyond time.

No hunter places a trap while the animals are watching. Like a hunter, negativity tries to catch you with traps of negative thoughts and feelings. But if you are in a state of observation—if you are *watching*—you catch negativity off guard. You know where the trap is, and you avoid the place. Then that negativity, having no energy to sustain itself, dissolves.

Observation

I call observation the key to letting go. When something disturbing shows up, and we *observe* it without reacting emotionally, we do not get thrown off balance. Remember, there is nothing going on that can touch your Spirit. Buildings may be falling down outside, but I still say nothing is going on. Why? Because it happened to the building, not to you.

Only human beings are capable of observing the presence of God in all things, including themselves. Human beings are sacred for that very reason. If only you could understand that simple fact, you would never need to read another self-help book! How can we observe God when we are observing resentment or worry? Where is God? God is in goodness. If you want to find God, don't waste your time with what is bad; spend your time in your goodness. Many people say, "I've been meditating for years and I haven't seen a damn thing. No fairies, no angels, no sparks, no nothing." I laugh. When we are impatient for results, we are not focusing on love. Love itself will let us know it is present and teach us *how* we should see it.

Once we focus on love, we are motivated by the very essence of life, not by some pattern of fantasies that causes us to think, "Oh, I wonder what she'd be like in bed. I wonder what he'd be like in bed. I wonder what kind of car they're driving. I wonder what we're going to eat tomorrow for breakfast. I wonder if I'll be able to get home before the traffic gets jammed up." Wonder, instead, what you are doing right now, because Divine presence is here.

Once you enter the Divine presence, you no longer worry about the past or the future. You are able to say, "Tomorrow? What is tomorrow? What's next week, what's next year? Does it matter if I am here or there? Wherever I am, I will be in this loving, radiant peace that illuminates all things."

We tend to focus upon our physical bodies, where they are, how they are feeling. People meeting me for the first time focus upon my face, my physical body and think that it is me. I get a big kick out of it. They've looked at my photograph, and when they meet me in person they are skeptical unless my face is the way it was in the photograph, gazing off into the skies. Just think what restrictions that puts on knowing ourselves and each other!

We experience the sensual pleasures of the body thinking they will awaken our Souls; but they awaken nothing but our ego. Becoming aware of this can be terribly painful. What do I do with that pain? I sit back and I say, "Wow, look at all that emotion inside of me. It is right across my shoulder and through my right ear." I don't try to explain it away, or be rid of it. I simply observe it.

We get our prejudices through our eyes. But when we truly *observe* the world around us, we find ourselves with fresh eyes: We are no longer encumbered with prejudice against the world. Often we say, "I like that one and I don't like that one." How do you know? "I looked at it." But did you observe it? "No, but I know what I like, don't I? Why should I observe?" Take another look. Because you wonder why you do not get what you want. The things you *do not* want are what you attract when you focus on your judgments, resentments, and guilts.

You may claim, as many do, that you are an intensely aware person. You are so intensely observing, forcing knowledge and awareness on yourself, that you forget to see the experience whole, and rise above it. Experience is valuable, but a dog can experience something and learn from its experience. Humans are able to get above the experience and observe it. They learn more from the observation than from the experience itself.

Have fun with observation. Lighten up. If every time you close your eyes, all you see is blackness, play a game with it. See what it looks like today. Observe what it does. Ask it if it is always black, or can it change color? The process of observing can be fun. People complain, "I close my eyes and I want to see God, I really want to, but He doesn't show up." Come on! You can't even control your own mind. Do you think you can control God?

Do not waste your time with such thoughts. Observe. Watch. See what happens.

Is observation starting to make more sense now? By observing, you can spontaneously rise into love. Spontaneously, without having learned how.

Watch out when you demand something of Spirit. Is it your ego or your ambition talking? Why don't you observe and see what part of you is really doing the demanding? By the time you find out, it will no longer matter. When we observe we rise in time above the desire, and we learn from being above it.

Meditation as Observation

Waking up means observing yourself to find out what you are doing. This is really the easiest process in the world. It is called meditation. People complain to me that they have been meditating for many years and all they see is darkness. They get irritated and angry. But remember, you don't have to *do* anything with that darkness. Get rid of your false expectations of what spiritual experience means: Just be silent and observe your darkness. If you could just realize it, God is speaking through the blackness that you see. But you are so busy being uptight and resenting it that you fail to hear God's voice.

As Spiritual Warriors, we do not *judge* the meditation. We do not judge the mind or the emotions. We observe them, and the observing itself dissolves our negative emotions. You may ask, what will be left when they are dissolved? If you ask, you are losing. But if we can observe what is happening and record it accurately, and then place the love in it, that love will move the disturbance. That is how we get free; that is how we dissolve negative karma.

Many of you have begun on your own the journey of the Spiritual Warrior, and have found that, totally spontaneously, something happened. You do not know yet what happened, but something occurred to lift you above yourself and bring you closer to God. I am trying to teach you what that was, and how to make that happen every time you meditate—to be as deep, as ecstatic, as God-intoxicated as you want to be.

Letting Go

I hope I have made it clear that the Spiritual Warrior never tries to control the guilt, the separation, and the rest. We observe them. Observation is a state of detachment, which lifts us into a greater awareness. We become more and more free.

When we leave that center of Divine awareness and go out in the world, we must go out as a participant observer. Going out is participating; the rest is observing. If you do not succeed at this the first time, don't worry. You are going to be given millions of opportunities to work at it: Namely, every moment of your life.

Have you noticed that when you try to work on guilt or resentment or other problems, they beat you on the head? We start by rationalizing our problems, and end up complaining about who is in our way, and how to get them out of the way, and if we had had better parents we would never have had any problems at all.... Then we say, "Why is my life so much harder than everybody else's?"

Why don't you sit back and observe your life? Now.

If you immediately get involved with your emotions or your thoughts of what should or should not be taking place according to some preconceived notion you have, you are creating a pattern inside of you that you will feel compelled to follow. So what we think is positive we attempt to put into our Soul, and what we think is negative, we try to send to hell and forget. But that is judgment. That is categorizing and placing. It has nothing to do with letting go.

If I could get you to observe with your mind and your ears for just 30 minutes, you would start transcending the limits of your personality. When we start to observe *without* judgment, the answer we have been seeking arrives naturally.

Meditation as Listening

It becomes a hard life when we pray to God for all sorts of help but we won't be quiet, sit back, and listen for the answers God provides. Don't dominate the conversation: Be silent and listen a little. In other words, *meditate*. Quiet down and observe your life. It is rare in meditation that you will hear anything. And when you do, more often than not, it is just your own mind chattering at you, and your meditation will seem fruitless.

What should you do then? My advice is; listen. What does your mind keep chattering to you about? If it says you didn't do the wash, then either get up and do it, or move past that thought. If you really want to meditate and see God, you will.

The only thing many people get out of meditating is calluses on their bottoms—and maybe not even that because they won't sit still long enough!

If this describes you, your meditation has taught you at least one useful thing: How *not* to do it. If 25 or 30 years of study have not brought you anything but this, you might want to consider a change.

Thinking you cannot change is not even horizontal thinking; it is perpendicular, and it is headed straight down.

Practice the discipline of holding your attention on a thought. It won't make you a slave; on the contrary, it will teach you how to be in control of it. When you can control, focusing your attention, you can free your mind. Observation is the key to doing this, and in fact this entire book is geared toward allowing you to free up your attention so that you can put it where you want it.

When you meditate, the ego wants to feel like it has accomplished something after sitting there all that time. But why give up your precious attention to your ego? That will just create defeat: Anxieties, animosities, depressions, insanities, and general craziness. Instead of allowing your ego to push you around, observe, then choose wisely where you will place your thoughts and actions.

Observation and letting go will ultimately lead you to a greater awareness of the reality of death, and a process of "letting God." And that is awareness of the joy that we are, the bliss that is present.

You do not have to sit and "space out" with some special posture, legs crossed, legs uncrossed, arms in the air, arms at your sides, and so on. You do not have to go around saying, "Oh, I'm so happy, everybody!" None of these external things really matter.

But when you attain contact with that Divine energy, you will be able to say, even in the midst of deep depression, "I'm so darn blissful the depression doesn't bother me anymore."

Think of it this way. You are on your way to visit your lover and there's a rock in your shoe. You know it's there, but that rock does not bother you because you are focused on getting to the one you love. You completely transcend the pain. That night when you get back home and you take the shoe off, there is the bruise on your foot. You say, "I wonder how I got that." But then you start dreaming about your lover, you forget about the pain again and you fall back into the bliss of your beingness.

Ego

We human beings are not islands in a vast, empty universe. If anything, we are just pebbles in the stream. What we think is our unique individuality is really an ego struggling to think it is God. It will never make it, of course; it is not even designed to make it. All the ego is designed to do is get you out of bed in the morning, to make you live in this world, to experience this world. It is for you to learn how to take that ego and put it aside when you are not using things in this world. The ego is not necessary to know God, to find God, to be aware of that which is. The ego gets in the way.

I have talked a lot about observation in this chapter. When we are observing, we are in that place that I call purity—purity of thought, of emotion, of content.

In that moment of feeling good, that moment of observation, the power of God will move inside of you. You're asking, is this some kind of phenomenon? Absolutely! And once you get a taste, you will be hooked: Hooked not only on your high, but also on your low, because that, too, is part of this energy of God.

Observing our beingness is the process that releases us and opens us and expands us to let the Spirit flow through us. Yes, it is a miracle, but if we try to partake of it through our egos, we block it. And so we have to maintain our openness. We have to say simply, "Lord, I receive, and I am grateful." It doesn't matter what religion you practice; we must all surrender to the highest source we can. All of us must ask for protection, for that is what surrender really is—placing ourselves into the protecting hands of God.

Secret of the Spiritual Warrior: Loving—The Highest Intention

Spiritual progression is not to be found outside, in the physical world. Spiritual progression is found inside you. Once your intention toward higher awareness is clear, you will begin to move up, instead of moving horizontally. You will see that your existence is not confined to this world. You will begin to live your everyday life in greater awareness of the now. The mistakes, the decisions, and the fantasies of yesterday will belong to yesterday, not today or tomorrow.

You cannot do anything wrong as long as you are acting with love and awareness. I have three ground rules that govern my life. I'll share them with you:

Don't hurt yourself and don't hurt others.

Take care of yourself so you can help take care of others.

Use everything for your upliftment, learning, and growth.

To some people these ground rules seem too simple, even simplistic. But think how your life would change if you lived them, *really* lived them! It may sound silly, but applying these rules to whatever you do really will guarantee a fulfilling life. Your Spirit will converge and you will live in higher awareness.

Chapter 4

Embracing the Petty Tyrant

In our training as Spiritual Warriors,
we want the critics.
We want a petty tyrant in our lives,
somebody who is able
to bug us with impunity,
because these people always show us
where we are going in relation to our intention.
As a result, they can help keep us
in line with our intention.

Most of us resist or try to avoid adversity. We try to get away from people we don't like, people who push our buttons and make us uncomfortable, or hurt our feelings. Carlos Castaneda has described these people as "petty tyrants." He explains how the purpose of these people is really to expose our sense of self-importance. This is a great way to look at things, and it is the way of the Spiritual Warriors: They see adversity as a blessing, as an opportunity to use *ruthlessness* and *impeccability* to grow spiritually.

Look for the petty tyrants in your life. They will urge you to the next level of your spiritual expression and help you discover a more beautiful way of living life. This doesn't mean you "use" people as tools for your own spiritual advancement. What you're using is the way *you* feel about your petty tyrants. When you learn to make use of your feelings, these people will no longer seem like petty tyrants in your eyes.

Petty tyrants can be our bosses, co-workers, neighbors; they can even be our spouses or our children. Sometimes a petty tyrant will be a person in your life who—no matter what you say to them, no matter how many attorneys you consult, no matter how many policemen you talk to—somehow seems to have a right to keep doing something over and over and over to you, at you or against you.

In our training as Spiritual Warriors, we want the critics. We want a petty tyrant in our lives, somebody who is able to bug us with impunity, because these people always show us where we are going in relation to our intention. As a result, they can help keep us in line with our intention.

Ultimately it is always our self-importance that throws us out of alignment with our spiritual intention. Self-importance is our greatest limitation. If you are asked to empty bedpans, and your self-importance tells you that you are destined for something far more glamorous than that, you are limiting your opportunities for spiritual expression. The good news is that even if you let your self-importance throw you out of alignment, you cannot be thrown out forever. You will come back into harmony and even grow from the experience of having been out.

So stop and listen to your petty tyrants for a moment. Recognize how much self-importance, righteousness, ego there is inside of you. Acknowledge your hate, your resentment. In this listening and acknowledgment, you are aligning yourself inside with your Spirit. And in this way, your petty tyrant is actually helping you converge your Spirit.

Petty Tyrants—An Exercise

Take some time to answer the following questions in writing. They will help you to focus on the areas inside yourself—inside your Spirit—that are affected by your petty tyrant. You may also want to ask a friend or spouse to read your responses and offer suggestions for handling your petty tyrant.

1. Identify a petty tyrant in your life, past or present.

2. How does the petty tyrant challenge your self-importance?

3. Describe what that self-importance is.

4. Instead of reacting negatively, how can you respond in a centered way?

5. Close your eyes and practice using ruthlessness, which is the Sword of Truth, the Sword of the Heart, to cut away the illusion. If you need to forgive yourself first, do it. (One way is to say to yourself, "I forgive myself for judging myself for . . .") When you experience the presence of Spirit inside of you, open your eyes.

6. When you finish, spend some more time writing: Reflect on your experience—what you've learned, and what you still need to do.

Completing this exercise thoughtfully may challenge you. But then, meeting challenges is part of becoming a Spiritual Warrior.

Secret of the Spiritual Warrior: Simplify and Relax

Be patient. Take a breath. Be aware of your shoulders. Lower them. Relax.

Whatever comes your way comes because you have brought it to you. The romantic way to look at it is to say you've been given a test, which you can pass or fail. In reality it is just you, drawing to yourself the next step in your growth. At this point you can go in whatever direction you want to go. It is easier to go negative because that is the thrust of our world. To choose positive or negative is not an equal contest. The odds are stacked against you. As a Spiritual Warrior, with your Sword of Truth and armed with your intention, the odds will tilt back in your favor.

But you must have the energy to do it. A Spiritual Warrior works with impeccability to conserve energy for the most important task of all: Awareness. Awareness means being open and continuing to expand in spite of and because of any obstacles you meet.

Simplify your life. You do not need all the clutter you are holding on to. Get rid of it now because it is stealing your energy.

The clutter in your life takes energy to maintain. Start with the smallest things. Clear away a little and you'll be amazed at the vast amounts of energy it releases inside of you. Incomplete things also tie up energy. Look at all your unread books, and declare them complete. Guilt—let go of it, right now.

Keep around you only the things that give you energy.

PART II

BECOMING A
SPIRITUAL WARRIOR

Chapter 5

Coming into Alignment

Inside us,

who we are as an eternal being

meets the person who is here temporarily.

Here the Spirit,

the emanation from God,

meets us,

the selves we know.

This is our point of convergence:

A point of concentration or attention.

As you work with the techniques in the first section of this book, you will find your awareness expanding and bringing new perspectives to what you previously considered commonplace experiences. This second section is designed to support you in these new responses, beginning with a concept I call "convergence."

If I had a blue bubble in one hand and a yellow bubble in the other, and I brought the bubbles together so that they touched, I would still have blue and yellow. But if I began to merge them, what colors would I have? I would get blue on one side, yellow on the other, and a new color—green—in the middle. That new blend in the middle is the point of convergence.

Inside us, who we are as an eternal being meets the person who is here temporarily. Here the Spirit, the emanation from God, meets us, the selves we know. This is our point of convergence: A point of concentration or attention. The Spirit can be converged inside us in many ways. Someone yelling at us can change our convergence. When Spirit and mind move to the left, we can be very irritated and yell back. But when they move to the right, we say "Aha!" We see the events of the moment more clearly, and new ideas come forward, often quite rapidly.

An essential part of your training as a Spiritual Warrior is recognizing when this takes place.

If we can change our spiritual consciousness, we can move toward the convergence point. We can spend more of our time in spiritual pursuit instead of just reacting to the material world. We can remain at peace. We can never control God, but we can align and flow with His will.

We cannot control the sun, either, but we can choose to stay inside or to go outside with sunscreen and plenty of water.

If we have a clear intention toward a spiritual pursuit and are reading uplifting material or meditating on that intention, Spirit and mind will begin to converge. We achieve a heightened state of awareness, of knowing. As the point of convergence turns, our perception—the way we see the world—turns with it. We actually look into the unknown. When our moments of convergence end, we won't remember anything, even though we understood it at the time. (This sounds as if I am describing early senility but, trust me, I am talking about the spiritual process.) We know something happened, but we can't quite put it together. Then when we return to the heightened state of awareness, that understanding returns to us, and we can't imagine how we could have forgotten.

It is easy to say, "Align yourself with Spirit," or "Get right with God," but it is difficult to do consistently. We get ourselves aligned, and then our point of convergence shifts. Suddenly, we are back in our habitual state. The thing to do is not to get discouraged but to pick up from that place and continue on.

Moving the Spirit Point

Let's look at it from a practical standpoint. You're reading a book and, depending on your intention toward the material, the words may converge your Spirit point and start to move it. If it moves on you too fast, you may drift into unconsciousness and then sleep. If it moves just about right, you flow with it and, in flowing, your perception of the material will trigger a whole set of secondary experiences in your mind. Things will become clearer and begin to fall into place. This, obviously, has very little to do with the book; instead it has to do with how the convergence point is moving through your body.

In this way you will gain a clear perspective, which will be very nice—for a while. Then your neighbor will make a loud noise, or your kids will scream, or your spouse will walk across the room, and you will fall back into the same old patterns, as if nothing had changed. What happened was that your convergence point moved back to its usual place and you saw the world from your habitual perspective. It is difficult to move the convergence point away from its normal place.

Moving your convergence point can be like trying to draw with your eyes closed: It is confusing and disorienting at first. It takes practice. And the more you practice, the better you will become at shifting. You can move your convergence point into another, higher awareness; and in that way, you can be free.

This brings us to one of the cardinal principles of the Spiritual Warrior:

It is not what is happening that is important; what is important is what you are doing with it. Thus the Spiritual Warrior says, "Regardless of what it looks like, regardless of my perception, I will use everything for my advancement, upliftment, and growth."

Maintaining Our Alignment

When your convergence point shifts and you are able to hold it, you open up new perspectives, awarenesses, and insights. But if you do not maintain it through impeccability, it starts to move back. There are no easy formulas to prevent this. Spirit is ruthless, not out of malice, but out of purposefulness. When we are moving in the same direction as Spirit (which we will know by checking inside with the part of us that is attuned to these things), we are aligned; when we go off on a tangent, Spirit goes right on without us; Spirit does not stop to accommodate us. We follow Spirit, not vice-versa.

As an analogy, suppose you are hired by a corporation. You are given a job description, a title, and a behavioral matrix to follow along the lines of the corporate culture. No matter how well you do in any one area, if you don't fulfill all three, you are let go. You may ask, "Why did you fire me with all the energy I've put into my job?" The answer is that you were not aligned with the company's goals. You may say, "That's not fair." They may say, "We are not dealing with fair; we are dealing with alignment of where we are going." So it is with Spirit.

Moving to a higher level of awareness can be a little disconcerting and uncomfortable. It is unfamiliar territory. You might wish to go back to where you were. It's easy to slip back, to feel secure, comfortable, and familiar. Believe it or not, some people call that freedom. But all it is is a comfortable prison. Going back means that you are not handling and integrating your alignment with the Spirit—which is continually moving.

Different Forms of Alignment

We can learn to recognize when we are aligned and when we are not. Physically, not being aligned will feel and look like tension; emotionally, like upset; mentally, like resistance. Let's examine some aspects of alignment.

Physical: When we are grumpy, we are out of alignment with ourselves. You may have found that if you wake up grumpy and you go back to bed for a nap, you can change your mood. The nap allows you to leave your body and then return straight and aligned.

Emotional: When you are out of alignment emotionally, you may find yourself being very reactive and impetuous, speaking without thinking. Simply sitting quietly, or practicing a breathing meditation, can bring you back into alignment. The old approach of counting to ten before saying something is actually a simple but effective way to realign the emotions and the mind. It breaks the momentum of the anger and allows us to respond to the situation instead of reacting to it.

Everything around us can teach us. The difficult thing is, often we prefer being the teacher to being the student. But we can only really become the teacher as we learn, gain experience, and then demonstrate what we have learned. The greatest teachers teach by example.

Mental: Being out of alignment at the mental level shows itself in more insidious and long-lasting ways. We can find mental alignment by reading a book that stimulates the intellect. But we will get into trouble if we read something and then parade it to others as our own experience. That is living in the false self, and this type of misalignment can last a very long time. Proclaiming things without having tested and experienced them is living in delusion. It's like reading a cookbook and then calling yourself a chef.

The same type of thing takes place when you live in what you think *might be* or *should be* true instead of living in your own personal experience. Effectively, you are conning yourself; you will feel cheated and may try to blame others when things don't go right. But if your words and your actions are truly in line, you can be sure you are living your own life and not someone else's.

It is a tremendous thing to have no separation between your Spirit and your mind, emotions, and body. Then there will be just one Spirit coming into convergence and alignment with the unknowable energy we call God.

Falling Out of Alignment

It is so difficult to reach perfect alignment, and so easy to fall out of it. We must never pause, look about us proudly, and make self-important statements like, "At last, wow, here I am! It took me so long and I studied so hard." That only makes the fall, when it comes, all the more discouraging. It is hard to try again when we are still worn out from our first exertions, but that is what the Spiritual Warrior must do. After you fall on your face a thousand times, you may be tempted to say, "I'm not going to get up again because I'll just fall." But you have to get up, even if it is just to avoid having people step on you.

Sometimes we allow other people to shake us. If someone calling himself a Buddhist or Moslem or Christian or Jew lays their belief structure and experience on you, along with their doubts about *your* experience and *your* belief structure, why should it bother you? Their way of aligning just has a different name on it. We are all striving for the same thing: To align ourselves with the Spirit, our Divinity. Why should we worry about their experience?

Once you decide to keep moving forward, you will devise a method to chart your progress. And gradually you will begin to move from what you know into what you don't know—the unknown. And when the unknown becomes the known, the unknowable becomes simply the unknown. Everything starts to move closer to you. It comes toward you as you go toward it. The past pushes you and the future pulls you—ultimately, to convergence and alignment. We can view it as predestined, and in a sense it is. But the time it takes is not. Eternities can feel like moments, and moments can feel like eons of eternities.

Chapter 6

Manifesting Your Spirit

When we define "manifestation" as
"appearing physically,"
we are only taking into account
physical forms, objects.
But successful manifestation is only complete
if it results in a change in consciousness.
That change of consciousness,
in turn,
is the realization
that the essence of what we sought in a physical form
is actually inside of us.
"Having" doesn't mean possessing a physical object.
It means no longer experiencing the need.

Most of you reading this book already have the basics of food, shelter, clothing, and love. Yet you probably still feel in need. You covet many things—particularly material objects (a car, a boat, a stereo, or even a chocolate cake). When you acquire what you covet, you feel great at first—for a few minutes, maybe even a few days, you're satisfied, thinking that you don't "need" anything else. But then, inevitably, you distance yourself from the thing you wanted, and you go on to coveting something else, still looking "out there" for something to fill your needs.

This cycle can go on forever unless you understand that when you covet something out there, you are really coveting yourself. And you can never find yourself out there. The very thing you are after—the *essence*—is inside of you all the time. And you don't have to leave the physical earth to find it.

What does "essence" mean? And how can it be inside of you? Even when you consume something (a chocolate cake, a car, or even a relationship) you have only consumed the *form*. It is like the shell of a nut without the kernel, and that is why forms can never, ever satisfy. What you are really searching for is the kernel, the *essence*, the interior sense of fullness and satisfaction. But as long as you are looking "out there" you won't find that essence. It is "in here," already inside of you. And it is by manifesting your Spirit that you gain access to that hidden essence. Only by manifestation do you bring it out and put it to work in your life.

But we must be careful about how we define "manifestation." When we define "manifestation" as "appearing physically," we are only taking into account physical forms, objects. But successful manifestation is only complete if it results in a change in consciousness. That change of consciousness, in turn, is the realization that the essence of what we sought in a physical form is actually inside of us. "Having" doesn't mean possessing a physical object. It means no longer experiencing the need.

Abundance Is a Process of Consciousness

Webster's Dictionary defines abundance as quantity, affluence, wealth. But in spiritual terms, abundance does not mean possession of objects. Rather, it means access to the essence of what all things are. It means being in communion with that essence inside of you. True abundance is this awareness of the whole, this satisfaction of all our needs (which are far fewer than we may think). That is abundance.

Not a million dollars. Not exotic cars. Those are only personality shows. Yet we constantly covet these "things," as if they can meet our needs. We become "rich"—but being rich, being wealthy, is not the same thing as abundance. Do you see the difference?

When the ego or personality looks at abundance, it sees quantity. The Soul views it differently. It sees *quality*.

If you have five hundred lovers and none of them genuinely loves you, there is no value in any of them. What looks like abundance is really emptiness. But if you have one person who is really present, loving and uplifting you, then you have everything. You possess all in one.

Abundance, therefore, is a consciousness, not a material scorecard. When we have abundance, everything we need is entirely present.

How do we achieve abundance? How do we find this essence which we already possess inside ourselves? Spiritual Warriors find what they are looking for by doing. Doing includes specific tasks like meditation and spiritual exercises, and it finally means precipitating down from the Spirit to manifest through the emotions, the intellect, and the body. When we have access to the essence we can share it with others, through manifestation. This chapter will bring you a little closer to that goal.

Levels of Spirituality

Once we have mastered silent, listening observation, we can more easily rise in our spiritual consciousness. The process of spiritual growth and expansion has often been compared to climbing a mountain. As one goes up and a new level is reached and secured, that level becomes the base station for climbing still higher.

But lest you get too comfortable at the base station, and forget that your job is to climb toward the peak, Spirit steps in. You begin to feel trapped, stifled, hemmed in; you may even wonder if you are going crazy. This is Spirit's way of driving you up to the next level.

Naturally there are always falls. Spirit may even kick

you down the mountain, to the level below. (As I said in the last chapter, Spirit can be ruthless!) You come back down looking like a nincompoop. You flounder around saying, "Oh, I don't know how to do this." Though getting pushed down a level in this way can be discouraging, this is how Spirit tells you that you've got more learning to do on that level; you didn't grasp it completely the first time. Now the challenge is to master it, then move on.

It takes time to reach perfect mastery, but most people are too impatient. They won't take time to 'listen' to the silence, to rise to the elevation necessary to observe a situation neutrally. Many people meditate this way: They sit down and if they are not entertained royally by Spirit within five minutes, they give up and start looking for a distraction. That is not the way of a Spiritual Warrior.

Of course, the other extreme does not work either, though I truly wish it did. I have spent whole existences sitting in a hole in the ground, not saying anything, waiting. But it's really not that difficult. If I had had someone already advanced in Spirit reach down, tap me on the shoulder, and say, "look, booby, just sitting there with your mouth shut doesn't seem to be doing much good. That's not correct action. It's something, and sure, you've got the right idea, but you're not *doing* anything with the right idea." Somewhere in between is the happy medium, where we take dynamic control of our own passivity, but at the same time give the Spirit room to act.

Remember that the levels of spirituality described above aren't magic formulas; nor are they scientific and precise, like a chemical reaction. When we try to calculate, to keep a tally on the good things in life, we become rigid and don't allow the highest good to reveal itself. Learn to be flexible, to stop counting, and to have God as your partner. Allow the Spirit to become manifest, but not in terms of your anxieties, your irritabilities, or your consciousness of time. Spiritual Warriors step outside of time and await the Spirit in patience.

I. Correct Identification

How do you know when you don't need something? As a rule, if you don't use it for six months to a year, it can go. Quite simply, we don't use what we don't have use for. Most people are so full with what they don't need that they have no space for the new. They are attached to how pretty something is or to its sentimental value or to how "desperately" they need it. So they live in their desperation instead of in the abundance of the supply. The Spiritual Warrior, on the other hand, is ruthless in letting go of this excess baggage. The Spiritual Warrior says: "Look, I know it's pretty. So what?"

We must remember that personality is form, and therefore limited. Our Soul, however, is formless. It is not limited to a single form, but can function through any form. Our great freedom as human beings is our ability to function *through* something instead of just functioning *in* it. Functioning through is freedom. How do we do this? First of all, we have to have correct identification. We have to know who we are. We have to know who God is. We have to spend time in silence, in the creative exercises of Spirit (for more on this, see Tool of the Spiritual Warrior: Spiritual Exercises, immediately following Chapter 7). We must be open. We must be willing to live life as it comes: Not living in the good as it comes or in the bad as it comes, but living *life* as it comes. We must learn to expand with it *regardless*, instead of contracting and rejecting the changes in our lives.

An example: I knew a man who prayed for a better job. But a better job did not come along and eventually he lost the job he had. He was angry, he didn't like it, and to say he went into contraction would be an understatement. After he had been off work for a while, a back problem that he had began to heal, and when he was well again he found a much better job than the one he had originally had. Only then did he realize that he could not have gotten the better job until his back had healed, because he was allowed to rest. Losing the first job was a blessing, an opportunity for expansion—but at the time he had angrily rejected it.

And this is the natural response. Instead of expanding, most people contract. They contract by resisting, by trying to push things out or push things away. When they can't get rid of them, they are left with frustration, and, in its more extreme form, disease. Have you ever tried to get a certain thought out of your mind? It keeps you awake. You struggle against it but the thought outlasts you. When you wake up in the morning, the thought is still there, like a heartache. To you it may seem that you have been fighting it. But you are really only *hating* it.

Why not simply observe that thought? Let it be where it is. Just say, "You know, you're a nasty old thought, and I recognize that you disturb me. What the heck? I think I'll go to sleep anyway." Spiritual Warriors take the path of acceptance and choose to manifest brand new things around them by meditating and out-lasting the chatter in their minds. They pull the energy of Spirit through and the obsessive thought can't last. The higher energy dissolves and disperses it.

II. Correct Imagination

Correct imagination means having a very clear and vivid idea of what you want to take place. The pictures you carry in your mind are more important than those you carry in your wallet because they *affect* what they depict, and you are held responsible for them. In other words, if you carry negative pictures, you get negativity. The key is to consider our needs in light of the energy they represent. This sounds complicated but it is very important. Don't just imagine what you think you need; be clear about where that need really comes from. Consider the essence of what is going on. Does that need support the intention of your life? Does it support you moving into completeness, into joy, into humor, into fulfillment? Rather than saying, "I need that boat, I need that house, I need that chocolate cake," visualize the true essence of your need.

Again, the first step is silence, meditation. Intuition starts to take place, and you recognize God as your source. I am not referring to the god of a tiny ego personality, the god of our lower levels of consciousness, but the real God.

One very important question to ask yourself is, "What is God telling me about this image?" Is this image bringing me hatred, yelling, dissension, upset? Is it suggesting quarreling and opinion? If so, you have probably come up against what your ego wants. As a Spiritual Warrior you need to get this very clear: "If I am with the all, then I am not in tension or in need. I know I am with all things. I do not feel lack or pressure. I am poised. I am silent, peaceful. I can deal with any form that comes my way and let it go. I am not bound to anything." This is correct imagination.

III. Correct Attunement

Tuning in to a station on the radio takes time, patience, and a fine ear. We have to apply the same care to our spiritual attunement. We tune into Spirit through our mind, our emotions, our imagination, and our physical bodies, so we have to achieve a working balance among all of them.

This means tuning in so that our minds, our emotions, our imaginations and our bodies are all present, all focused on the one goal. Then the Soul says, "it's done." And the mind says, "It's done." The emotions say, "It's done." And the body says, "Yes," and takes action.

When we have this correct attunement, irresistible energy flows into the subconscious and radiates out. Other people feel this energy and are attracted to it. This is attunement.

Inventions are also brought forward this way. A person can be inventing something and go to bed with a great deal of enthusiasm for it. It hits the subconscious of the human race, and another person on the other side of the planet precipitates it down and starts inventing exactly the same thing. This is why these things seem to spring spontaneously all over. Once an idea comes, it will manifest to the most open channel. Inventors are the type of people who are open because they are curious for new learning. We should be like inventors because with that openness we can practice correct attunement.

Of course, correct attunement also includes being in harmony with your environment. That means not contributing to pollution, not destroying things without being aware of the consequences. It means not leaving things in a mess. It also means the ability to work with authority and to work as an authority, which means accepting your responsibilities and your commitments. You have, for example, assumed both responsibility and authority with the job you've chosen: So *work it*. Bring all your actions into attunement.

IV. Correct Action: True Manifestation

Finally, you will need correct action. Correct action means the willingness to do whatever is necessary— physically, emotionally, mentally—to make it all happen. Spiritual Warriors manifest themselves through correct action, because their only true intention is spiritual growth, expansion, and revelation. Whatever else comes is a bonus, to be enjoyed, to participate in, but never to get caught up in. Make the Spiritual Warrior way of acting your own, and you will begin to manifest the fruits of your spiritual progress in everything you do.

We manifest, not by trying to attract *to* us, but by expressing *out* from us: Not taking, but giving. When we are sharing that essence in our Soul, the genuinely good things come to us automatically—you don't have to manipulate, play the games, con somebody, or lie to them. The manifestation just starts taking place, and people are attracted to it.

Correct action does not mean that things are going to drop into your lap. You have to work for them—work to grow, work to expand, work for the next revelation. Many people won't move an inch unless they get paid for it. They are trapped. But the Spiritual Warrior says, "I'm doing this to grow, to expand. I'm taking on more responsibilities, not for more money, but for more growth, more ability, more knowledge." With that attitude you cannot be stopped. That is part of how you storm the gates of Heaven.

We cannot demand or assume that life will take care of us. That is taking a position. People who get stuck on a position are frozen. They are chained to their needs, their anxieties, and their desire for gratification. If you insist that someone is supposed to do something for you, you have chained yourself to that. Do you want those chains for your lifetime breakfast, lunch, and dinner? Spiritual Warriors do not fall into the trap of making their gratification and security depend on other people. The Spiritual Warrior goes for freedom.

Never forget that we are more than what we do. We are more than anything that we teach. We are more than what we say. We are more than we could ever express. Always keep in mind that the highest good will prevail and your main job is simply to cooperate with it. It's ironic, but that is the key to being truly in control—cooperation.

Aligning the Four Correct Actions Into Spirit

When we find ourselves out of balance or cut off from the Divine, it is always because we are blocking ourselves. As hard as it may be to believe, no one else is blocking you! If you sit back and just observe the thing you feel is blocking you, you will realize that it is *your* creation. Then you will be able to move back into that loving neutrality.

Observe yourself, identify all that is not part of you. Then be ruthless in letting those things go, simply by no longer participating in them. Release and disperse them. What is left? The Soul. You.

With correct identification, correct imagination, correct attunement, and correct action, we recognize the essence of what we seek; we precipitate that energy down, and manifest it in what we do. We recognize and embrace our abundance, always keeping ourselves open to the highest good.

Talking about this is simple. But it takes practice to master it. The Spiritual Warrior always returns to the same basic principles. Take back your inner territory that you gave away to what is not you. Set your goal and then follow through ruthlessly. You may attempt to manifest out of Spirit 500 times, and fail. But what if when you get to number 501 it all snaps into place?

Will you get bored doing this? Maybe, if you go back to the old definition of manifestation which locked you into physical form and made you the prisoner of *matter*.

It is your choice. When you finally do what works you will look at all the good things in your life and say, "Wow, look at everything that's happening. I haven't done anything." But you have: The years of good, solid exercise in Spirit—the correct identification, imagination, attunement, and action—have led you to that essence within you. It doesn't happen by chance. It is very hard to accidentally align with the four correct actions into Spirit.

Chapter 7

Moving from the Unknown to the Unknowable

The mind stops
at the limit of the mind;
the emotions stop
at the limit of the emotions;
the imagination stops
at the limit of the imagination.
This may seem obvious,
but it is amazing how many people
think that they can use their emotions
to solve mental problems
and that they can use their minds
to find God.

Many of you, reading this book, are hoping to come to a deeper awareness of God. You have preconceived notions of what the Divine will look like. But the reality of God cannot be learned through study. The only way you can know God is through direct experience inside of you. And when you do find God, I can guarantee He won't be floating through the air saying, "Whoo, whoo." God is not phenomenon. God is God. Spiritual Warriors realize they will never know God in the same way they understand thoughts or facts, because God is in the unknowable.

There are three categories of knowledge: First, what you know—the known; second, what you don't know but can know—the unknown; and third, what you can never know—the unknowable.

The known is what is *here*, what is visible; I call it functional reality or empirical evidence. It is the basis from which all history, all mythology takes place. It is also the basis of all the external events of our lives. We all have an immense amount of knowledge about this known world. But this knowledge, more often than not, goes for nothing in matters of Spirit. You would think that we would live righteous, Spirit-filled lives in a familiar, comfortable place, because we would know exactly what was right and proper. But isn't it amazing—we use our knowledge of what is right and proper to corrupt ourselves. We eat foods we know will give us heartburn (or worse); we say things to our husbands, wives, or loved ones that we know will result in an argument. We all know what to do to make our lives healthier and better, but we don't do it!

Moving from the Unknown to the Unknowable

The unknown, on the other hand, is strange and unfamiliar territory. It is full of promise, full of hope, yet at the same time almost terrifying, since we are afraid of wandering astray. When we enter the unknown we are entering our own ignorance, and so we can go only one step at a time.

It is so important to recognize clearly where our knowledge ends and our ignorance begins. How can we learn unless we admit we need to learn? To teach others what we do not know fully ourselves is dangerous and destructive work. It prevents us personally from advancing and places sometimes insurmountable obstacles in the way of others. Spiritual Warriors cannot reach their goal by acting as stumbling blocks to others; they know they will never advance by hindering others. The search for God, remember, is not a race toward a finish line.

As for the unknowable, it can be said, "God is unknowable, but I know God." How can that be true? How does a person recognize God? The answer is: As best he can. Some people take what they know about God and immediately start preaching it so they can get more people going in one direction. This gives the illusion that God is a *known* quality. As a result, people cease to seek inwardly, having the idea that because many people are following a particular way, it must be right. But that is a fallacy. Nothing in the world can relieve us of our personal responsibility for seeking the truth. How can something as noble as religion get us into so much trouble? Because we constantly confuse what we know or think we know, with what is *truth*. The Spiritual Warrior has to be able to discern the difference.

The Left and Right Sides of Spirit

The information that follows may seem rather abstract. It's okay if you don't fully understand it. Just allow your inner wisdom to absorb it. Keep reflecting on the issues suggested here. You will find your understanding of them deepening more and more as you progress toward Spiritual Warriorhood.

Alignment doesn't happen in the known, because in the tangible, everyday world there is no such thing as perfection. We all want to be first, and being first is not alignment. Spiritual Warriors are basically indifferent to their *place* in the world. They are content where they are, and say, "the position I am in is the best position for my learning, for my growth, and for my expansion."

Neither can we align in the unknown, the area of our darkness and ignorance.

Out of the unknowable alone comes spiritual alignment for all of us on this planet. Our intention as Spiritual Warriors is to get in alignment. And how does it come about? Not in knowing but in *awareness*. We come into awareness of the unknowable. But how can we become aware of it? By coming into alignment with it.

In the left and the right sides of Spirit, we find known and unknown. The following list breaks down roughly the qualities associated with these two sides of the Spirit. Remember that both sides are necessary to maintain the balance of Spirit.

Moving from the Unknown to the Unknowable

Aspects of the Left Side and the Right Side

Left Side	Right Side
Feminine	Masculine
Dark	Light
Passive	Active
Soft	Hard
Intuitive	Logical
Emotional	Intellectual
Creative	Destructive
Natural	Synthetic
Earth-centric	Spirit-centric
Abstract	Tangible
Path away from God	Path toward God

Only through the right side can you go into the unknowable and have alignment with it. If you go into the left side you go into a quagmire of universes in your consciousness that will pull you down. The left side is undefined, unformed Spirit. It is what has been referred to as a hell. You will recognize the left side because it wants power and force. Power and force are wasted energy. But on the right side are strength and endurance. The Spiritual Warrior impeccably chooses these cooler, more recollected qualities. Power and force wear out in a moment, but strength and endurance last forever. (For more on the left and right sides of consciousness, see the next chapter.)

Insecurity and the Illusion of Comfort

It's not easy to live on this planet, simply because you

have to keep living here, and living here, and living here. And some part of you says, "I'm tired." Only God can release you, refresh you. But in order to win this freedom, you have first to surrender to the unknowable, which is Spirit.

People want to approach the unknowable in their own way, and that ego intention moves their awareness out of alignment into the left side. They remain bound to the earth and they can spend eternities wandering around in the illusions of their own consciousness. They are suspended there, totally closed off to higher influences. It is easy to be caught in this way because it is such a *comfortable* trap. The left side will keep you struggling because it is very deceptive. Being in the left side looks effortless, but don't fool yourself. Our unwillingness to move, unwillingness to change, and unwillingness to grow are constantly interrupted by feelings of insecurity, depression, despair—which, if we could only read them right, are prompting us to change, to discover true alignment. And when that alignment comes, and we suddenly step out of the trap, we cry out in amazement, "Oh, my God, I'm alive, I want to be alive!"

Approaching Awareness

The division between the two sides of Spirit is so delicate, it can take years of experience to learn to recognize the subtle energies emanating from the two sides. And so many people deafen themselves to Spirit by addictions; physical, mental, emotional. Addiction is a way of locking oneself into the left side of consciousness, and cutting off the possibility of movement.

Imperfection is part of being human, and none of us is completely open to the movement of Spirit. But the Spiritual Warrior must come to a place of no judgment. If we are on a ship of fools, let's at least make sure that we keep sailing.

To make that sailing smoother, do yourself a big favor: Stop being a spoiled child; turn your spoiledness into the Warrior's readiness. Spoiledness is left-sided energy. Demands and addictions are left-sided energy. Use them as preparation to step forward into something new. Start to change the neurological and physiological patterns which were discussed earlier. See where the alignment energies are coming in. These energies don't obey any rules; it's up to you to use them to advance your spiritual intention.

Alignment with Spirit involves detachment from the world; but it does not mean hatred of the world. The joy of alignment flows over into everything you do, including the most mundane aspects of your day-to-day life. How few people realize that it is actually easier to live in alignment through the right side, by loving, caring, and sharing. You automatically touch others. You don't have to search them out or puzzle over how to help them. It just takes place.

This is not to say that alignment with Spirit is not an ongoing challenge. But remember, your intention sets your direction, and as long as you are moving in the direction of your intention, you are doing all you need to. There is no need to make excuses, no need for apologies, just do what you can do.

It has been said by the Spirit that not one Soul will be lost. It doesn't say how long it will take you to get there! These are things for you to ponder. Observe yourself; see what pulls you to the left side, and what pulls you to the brightness of the right side.

We constantly ask *how* and *why*, but we won't stop and listen long enough to hear the answer. The answer sits inside of us. In fact it has been sitting there so long that we don't recognize it because it has become familiar. Alignment helps us to find all the forgotten answers. When you are aligned with Spirit, you are left, not with information, but with clarity.

Knowing by Doing

By this point you know that being a Spiritual Warrior means putting everything you come up against to good use. You can use everything in your life to advance awareness, and the left side can be used as a guidepost showing you where not to go. If you turn your back to the black darkness of the left side, then both sides become open to you. Then you can move straight ahead as a Spiritual Warrior and, at some point, the unknowable will engulf you—not as a thought or as a feeling, but simply as it is.

When we come out of a dark room into a bright sunshiny day, we have to shield our eyes until they adjust to the light. Spirit is like that light. You move toward Spirit, but you can only go as far as you can endure its brightness. Then you must adapt and align yourself with the brightness and fill yourself with that brightness so you can then move on to the next level of brightness.

When it gets too bright, you will be tempted to turn away from the light, but that only leads to despair and heartache and sorrow. I have been there many, many times. I know that many of you who are reading this have been there as well.

The only way to avoid despair is to keep facing the light no matter how it hurts our eyes. We cannot approach the unknowable in terms of the mind, because the mind stops at the limit of the mind; the emotions stop at the limit of the emotions; the imagination stops at the limit of the imagination. This may seem obvious, but it is amazing how many people think that they can use their emotions to solve mental problems and that they can use their minds to find God.

These elements of consciousness are just tools. Tools need a guiding hand to do their work correctly. And that guiding hand needs to be a loving one.

Imagine for a moment a tremendous canvas hung in a narrow corridor. You can only look at a bit at a time. As you shift your eyes, the part you are looking at is known and the rest of the picture is unknown. You will never see the picture in its entirety; and so it is unknowable. Yet you do know it intimately, in fragments. In the same way, Spirit, the unknowable, becomes in a manner *known* to you, though its fullness remains forever unknowable.

The Spiritual Warrior deals in experience. When you have experience with God, you will realize that God is existence, and that in reality, you don't live God as much as God lives you.

If you look at a road map of how to get from New York to Jasper, Canada, you'll see just a series of markings on a piece of paper. Jasper is unknown to you. You can sit and look at that map forever, but it will never physically take you there. But once you get in your car and drive, the map becomes a reference point of what really exists. And seeing what is really there lets you know the accuracy or inaccuracy of the information on the map. After you have been over the territory and experienced it for yourself, you see how it fits together. Then you can trust the map enough to give it to someone else and say, "This can get you there." Spiritual Warriors follow the map to its outermost edges, testing and experiencing all for themselves.

So remember that what has been written here is unknown to you and you can't trust the unknown. You can have a sort of faith in it, a sort of hope in it, a sort of belief in it, but you cannot yet trust it until you do it and it works. Since Spiritual Warriors are always looking for challenges to take them to the next level of strength and awareness, knowing yourself and being able to trust yourself is essential, because you will be going into dimensions where you will be the only reference point.

Maintain Awareness

If you practice the inner work of meditation, contemplation, prayer, and spiritual exercises, all this will gradually become familiar, and the way of the Spiritual Warrior will become second nature to you.

Align yourself by training your attention on your intention; the convergence will shift in its own time. But always remember, you have fallen asleep once. Do not fool yourself—you can fall asleep again. If the awareness is not maintained, you will lose alignment, and so you will lose your sense of the presence of God. You will feel a yearning inside you, a loneliness even when you are with people; you will feel alienated and separated, as if you are not a part of what is going on.

But you cannot be permanently alienated and separated from what dwells within you. Realign yourself by looking into yourself and loving yourself. Then love God and love your neighbor. That in itself is the greatest alignment.

Tool of the Spiritual Warrior: Spiritual Exercises

Spiritual exercises (s.e.'s) are designed to help us break through the illusions of the lower levels and move into an increased awareness of the Soul. Doing s.e.'s is an active technique of bypassing the mind and emotions by using a spiritual tone to connect to the energy that flows from God.

The only wrong way to do s.e.'s is not to do them, so there are no rules, rituals, or postures that are necessary to begin your practice. S.e.'s are an action of the heart, in which the approach is one of devotion and a clear intention to know Spirit and God in a greater way.

Having said that, for those people who would like to have some form of methodology so they can begin their s.e.'s, here is a step-by-step procedure as a suggestion for doing fifteen minutes of s.e.'s.

1. Find a quiet place with low lighting and a comfortable chair to sit in. It is best not to listen to music while doing s.e.'s.

2. Sit upright, and close your eyes.

3. Say a brief prayer asking for the Light of the Holy Spirit for the highest good, and ask

for protection and guidance during your s.e.'s.

4. Chant the Hu (pronounced h-u or hue) or the Ani-Hu (ah-nigh-hue), which are sacred names of God. It is preferable to do this silently.

5. While chanting, focus your attention in the area near the center of the head directly back from your forehead. It is in this place that the Soul has its seat and the Soul energy gathers.

6. After you have chanted for about five minutes, stop and listen within. You are listening for the sound current, the sound of a vibration of God, which is very subtle. You may hear it the first time you do this, or it may take years of practice. It is a very individual matter.

7. If you find your mind wandering and you lose the focus of listening, you can focus the mind by chanting again.

8. After about five minutes of listening, you can either continue to listen and look inside or return to chanting again. The times are approximate. The idea is to spend time in s.e.'s both chanting and listening.

9. If you see the color purple coming from the right or center of your head, you can allow

yourself to follow this inwardly, for this is a form the energy from the highest source of Light and sound takes when it is awakening people to an awareness of their Soul. This is known as the Mystical Traveler Consciousness. If the color is coming from the left side, we advise not following it because this is often a negative influence. (All this applies to seeing inwardly.)

10. After about five minutes more, you can open your eyes. You may want to wiggle your fingers and toes to bring the energy back into your physical body.

So ends your fifteen-minute session of s.e.'s. Through daily practice, you can gradually build on this time period until you reach the recommended time of two hours a day. For longer periods of s.e.'s, you can expand the time for chanting and listening to fifteen minutes each. For example, in an hour session of s.e.'s, you can chant for fifteen minutes, listen for fifteen minutes, and then repeat the chanting-and-listening cycle one more time.

All of the above are guidelines, and it is important to remember that the only wrong way to do s.e.'s is not to do them. So you can experiment with how you do s.e.'s, using what works for you at a particular time and not getting too attached to a certain form. And, again, the focus is on doing your spiritual exercises with as much loving and devotion to God as you can.

Chapter 8

Bridging the Left and Right Sides of Consciousness

The purpose of this discussion
is not to talk about the separation
between left and right sides,
but to bring you to the oneness of the side you are in.
Then you will straddle the line automatically
because you will see the rightness and its value
and the leftness and its value.
The Soul is both.

In chapter six, I compared the process of spiritual growth and expansion to climbing a mountain. As we reach each new level, we are tested before we can climb to the next, higher level. The struggle to maintain balance between the left and right sides of Spirit is one way we get tested. The passive or negative qualities of the left side test us to see if we really mean what we profess; they test whether our 'spiritual house' is built on rock or sand.

Every time you have made a resolution to do anything, from going on a diet to doing spiritual exercises every day, the negative power will come in and challenge you to demonstrate how much you meant it. In a way the left side plays devil's advocate inside of us: For Spiritual Warriors, its testing, doubting, holding back are essential, because they show us where we are going; they help us to define our intention, and they make us work for it. It is for this reason that you must maintain contact with both left and right in order to be spiritually whole. To deny one or the other is to deny part of yourself.

But Spiritual Warriors must not follow the left-sided path. A metaphor for this is the calf of gold in the time of Moses where, at the foot of Mount Sinai, it was worshiped even though it was a false idol. The left-sided path enters into fertility rites, and ends up being called witchcraft, or Wicca, or white magic. It turns into black magic when the male form tries to take over again and suppress what he says the female form did to him. And so we have the battle of the sexes, male against female.

Male and Female

Some people feel there is a missing link in their lives, hindering alignment, preventing them from moving forward in a more powerful way. The man feels he cannot come into alignment until he has a perfect relationship with a woman. The woman feels she will be incomplete until she has a perfect relationship with a man. We human beings constantly try to substitute relationships with each other for the relationship we are really longing for—a relationship with God.

There have been very few teachings that declare that the man is to gain his identity through the right side and into God. How many teachings dare to say to women, "Do not go to the man because you will pull him down. He wants to have sex with you so he can know himself through your body. If you accept him, all his doubts, fears, and worries will seem OK."

It can be more difficult being in a female form because—and you have to understand how this is being said so that you don't take umbrage with it—the female has always leaned toward the left-sided consciousness. Over the centuries, through the traditional teachings of mother to daughter, the dimensions of the left-sided energy have actually increased.

Men get fascinated by this left-sided energy, because their own right side sometimes gets boring. Instead of turning into the higher consciousness of the right side, men look for a member of the female gender. As they move closer and closer to her through courting, they tend to lose the identity of the right-sided energy field. They know their identity only through the woman, or the left-sided energy. And so we get the fall of man from the spiritual consciousness into the material. He falls and is caught by the woman, who then becomes his savior. He learns his identity through femininity, or left-sided energy.

Sensing he has fallen, he is not OK with himself, so he wants sex again and slips off to the left side. Instead of finding the validation he wants, he produces children, and then says, "Oh! Look how wonderful the children are! And they're mine." And he tries to pull them to the right side, but his wife won't let him. Why? Because they are her kids. They came out of her body. What did he do, except use his penis? It sounds crude, but is it done any other way?

If you look back through society, you can see it very clearly. Men, to attain their identity, have looked at the female form with its finery, and have judged it against their own comparative crudeness and coarseness. Yet the man's coarseness is really just a rebellion against his own female form. But he doesn't have to rebel. All he has to do is walk his path. No one has ever told him that. They've only told him about fear of death and going to hell. So the man's identity as a spiritual and sexual being within the energy field that is the body, has been lost to him and he doesn't know how to recover it. He promiscuously "screws the world," hoping to find somebody who will finally say, "You are it."

It's been basically the same situation for women: The way our society works, the woman longs to achieve the right-sided energy through a man. But women have to go across to the right side and get the energy, bring it back, balance it, and then go up. Men have to go across the left-sided energy, bring it back, and then go up.

This is not a popular subject. People will use their egos to doubt or negate these facts. But that doesn't change anything. Ultimately, the thing you are always dealing with is this: What are you doing with your energy? You can be in the left-sided energy, and be the oneness to yourself, and as soon as you hit oneness, you enter into the fullness of Spirit.

Be Whole Unto Yourself

I have met so many people who pray desperately for a man or woman to come along—usually a wealthy, good-looking man, or a wealthy, beautiful woman. They are so sure that this person is what they need that they never stop to ask themselves what they really need, and where this desire is coming from. I tell people: It is far more to the purpose to pray for enlightenment, to see God and to be filled with the Holy Spirit and to walk in God's Light; since true happiness, true abundance, comes from God and not from human beings.

The Spiritual Warrior, without rejecting the other sex, recognizes that each Soul has within itself all the elements of completeness. No other person can give us the perfect wholeness that comes from God. How difficult it is to accept this fact! We so easily make ourselves emotionally and even spiritually dependent on other people, including (and especially) those we love the most. Union with God requires a certain aloneness, and this can be frightening. It takes *work* to be whole unto yourself, to seek your energy and love in God rather than in relationships. It is only when both man and woman are spiritually whole that they are able to live in joy and genuinely sustain each other. Only when each member of the relationship takes responsibility for his or her own relationship with God can they find the true relationship that God intends men and women to have.

Does this mean men and women cannot grow together spiritually? Not at all. But even when a man and woman take this journey together, they must take it *separately* at the same time. One cannot carry the other. Each is a Soul, and each has to be prepared to be alone with God.

Balance and Oneness

The Spiritual Warrior walks in openness, learning from both the left and right sides. And we learn about the negativity of the left without having to go into its realm to do it. We learn about the right side without falling into self-righteousness and vindictiveness. We walk on both sides of this narrow path—and it *is* a narrow path.

The purpose of this discussion is not to talk about the separation between left and right sides, but to bring you to the oneness of the side you are in. Then you will straddle the line automatically because you will see the rightness and its value and the leftness and its value. The Soul is both.

We align our Spirit from both sides. When both are balanced there is perfect equilibrium, like a battery, where positive polarity and negative polarity are equalized. If you lean too much to either side, you will lose that balance. Pray from the center of Spirit.

Study your feelings and thoughts and your persuasions and your attitudes. The great teachers have said, "Know yourself" and "To your own self be true." Knowing what you are and being true to that is a fundamental stepping-stone into reality. But how can you step into reality if you are living in fantasy? Know that both forces hold power. The female is not necessarily weakness. The male is not necessarily strength. And we each contain elements of both.

The Soul is both male and female or neither, whichever way you care to look at it. In fact, it is a lot more than both or neither. It is part of Divinity. So it is also rocks and trees and ants and snails and water and clouds and snow and rain, not in their physical form but in their essence.

So getting stuck on male or female is a distraction. Stay clear of anything that suggests to you, "I can't seek God until—until I have a wife, until I have a husband, until I have kids, until my kids grow up, until my next lifetime, until I'm a different person"—and so on. God is for each of us, now, as we are.

It is necessary to accept the left side and the right side for what they are, and, at the same time, to integrate them. So we are constantly trying to balance.

If your intention is to awaken to yourself, then you must balance the male and the female

energy of the right and the left sides of your Soul. There is no perfect or permanent way to do this. We all fall and we always will, as long as we have a physical body. But so what? How often you fall is not important; what matters is how fast you can pick yourself up.

Secret of the Spiritual Warrior: Letting Go

If you want to change anything or anyone, change them inside yourself. Inside of you is the only place you can change anything. That is where everything lives. You carry the whole world with you wherever you go. A well-known Buddhist tale beautifully illustrates this truth.

Two monks approach a rushing river where there is a beautiful woman stranded, unable to get across. The monks have vowed not to touch women yet one of them picks her up, carries her across, and puts her down on the other side of the embankment. The other monk is very disturbed by this but says nothing. His disturbance builds and three days later he expresses his upset to the first monk. "We have vowed not to touch women yet you carried that woman across the river." The monk hears him to the end, then calmly replies, "I carried her across the river and set her down. You have been carrying her for three days."

From time to time you may find yourself feeling angry with people who have upset you in the past. Some of these people may be dead; others you will probably never see again; still others you say you have forgiven. The argument has ended; the fight is over; and yet it is still echoing within you. You are carrying your disturbances within

you, and keeping them alive with your energy.
The Spiritual Warrior learns to let go. Just let go.

Chapter 9

Stalking the Spirit

In the worlds of Spirit there is no time.
However, in this world,
time is a precious commodity.
This physical world is a springboard for you
into the higher consciousness.
Our bodies, minds, emotions, unconscious, and Soul
come together in one place
giving us the best opportunity in the universe
for growth and upliftment.

The most difficult thing about being a Spiritual Warrior is confronting yourself. It is in those moments when you are free from the distractions of the physical world that you have the greatest chance for upliftment. Take every chance you get because you will live in this world, get married, have kids, spend your life in slavery to car payments and house payments, work eight hours a day, and die—and you can take none of that with you.

The only thing that you can take with you—the only thing that is going to live, and never die—is the Soul.

As has been said many times in this book, the Spiritual Warrior must get this one intention very clear: "I'm keeping my eyes on You, Lord, only You." That means I am only doing the things that bring me closer to the Lord regardless of any distractions that may present themselves. Getting your intention clear and anchoring it inside of you is the essence of Spiritual Warriorhood. So, be purposeful. Not serious, but with purpose regarding what we are doing here. The religious path is serious, and the spiritual path is sincere—and is filled with joy and laughter.

As we have already learned, Spiritual Warriors have the Sword of their Heart in front of them. They use awareness as their primary weapon, and their armor is their intention. If your intention is to be loving and caring, that means you cannot let anything that is not loving or not caring come in.

Choose your intention carefully and then practice holding your consciousness to it, so that it becomes the guiding light in your life. Many times we put off things and promise ourselves that we will do them later. It is because we think that we will always have the luxury of time that we are so ready to put things off. But for the Spiritual Warrior, now *is* later: We live in awareness of our own deaths, and so, without hurrying, without rushing from one thing to another, we still endeavor never to waste a moment that might have been spent seeking God.

Imagine, just for a moment, that tomorrow is the last day of your life. What feelings does that thought bring up inside you? In order to be a Spiritual Warrior, from this moment on you will need to be aware of the possibility and the certainty of death, and come to terms with it.

That means that most of the things you tend to focus energy on are going to begin to seem meaningless. Getting, spending, seeking, standing in line; headlines, deadlines, stress, and anxiety: All of these are diminished by the thought of death. The beauty of death is its freedom. What do you care what people think when you are dying? What do you care about success or failure? As you focus on your death, you will begin to focus on your priorities; on what is really important.

There is an old cliché that asks, "If you had only one day left on earth, how would you want to spend it?" Perhaps it's a silly question, but it's worth spending some time thinking about it.

Since we don't know the moment we are going to die, so we can forgive ourselves and pray

and focus on God at the moment of death, we'd better start doing it now.

Are you starting to see how precious is the time you've already had? And how much more precious is the time that remains to you? Keeping death in mind is not being morbid. It's being aware, as a Spiritual Warrior, that you do not have time to waste.

Perhaps you can see now why you don't have time to do anything other than focus on your purpose or intention. If anything else matters to you, this is an opportunity to see what that is. As a Spiritual Warrior you do not have time to waste. Of course, as a regular human being you have as much time as you want. Humans prefer to focus on the uncertainty of their life and worry about it, rather than look at the one thing that is certain: Death.

Whether you like it or not, the bottom line always comes back to you. Whether you find failings in others or blame someone else because of a job you didn't get, because of your financial concerns, or your lack of fulfillment, in time it always comes back to you.

True wisdom lies in accepting your responsibility now, instead of waiting for time to change things, to correct things, to prove you right.

So take a moment right now to look at what your intention is as a Spiritual Warrior. You may want to ask yourself these questions (other relevant questions will suggest themselves to you as well):

Is there anything I have left undone or unsaid?

What are my incompletions?

How can I bring them to completion before I die?

Many times what you are involved in is wrapped up in memories that keep dragging you back to the past. Completion does not necessarily mean being finished physically. You can declare something completed by just saying, "It's done. I'm not going to do it anymore. It's finished just as it is."

When you fail to declare things done, a feeling of incompleteness keeps burdening you, draining off a little more of your energy every time it comes up. You may be going down the road, doing fine, feeling good, and all of a sudden some incident from the past comes up and grabs your attention. You say, "Oh, no! Where did that come from? I haven't thought about that in years. Now I feel terrible."

Do yourself a favor: Take a look at yourself now. Don't necessarily do anything, but *look* at yourself. What do you need to finish? What do you need to let go of? When you have totally forgiven yourself and others, you will have the full armor of God around you and in you; you will be able to walk through this world in God's armor, not battling anybody, but walking. Move on with determination, sometimes with stubbornness, but always in full armor. You will find that fears and guilts of the past will be powerless to hurt you.

Ruthlessness and Impeccability

Watch your "self talk"—what you tell yourself. Find some quiet time and listen to yourself. If negativity surfaces in the form of fears and doubts, challenge it. You know from experience that it cannot harm you. What is real is you, and that can never really be threatened or hurt.

John-Roger

You are probably thinking that you'll have plenty of time to think all this over, and that you'll be a Spiritual Warrior another day. Welcome to the human race. Observe the slow evolution of human beings. Sure, we have advanced enormously technologically, but as a race we are still doing the same destructive things that were reported in the Bible thousands of years ago. Our thinking that we have all the time in the world prevents us from maturing. Procrastinating is like pollution: It's wasteful and sloppy and depletes your energy.

You may have thought, picking up this book, that Spiritual Warriors would be feisty and combative, easily destroying all the obstacles in their path with a type of psychic kung-fu. But by this point we've all realized that Spiritual Warriors are not combative at all; they are as patient as they are feisty; and the battle they are fighting is far more difficult than any physical contest. Take away the limitations you have placed on how the Soul can function. The Spiritual Warrior can do anything. If you have decided to be a spiritual bushido or samurai warrior, you're limiting yourself.

When people ask me what a Spiritual Warrior looks like, I say, "Just like you." It is what you are doing inside of you while you participate outside of you—a totally simple way of living, an internal harmony and balance.

The Spiritual Warrior does not draw conclusions or take positions which then need to be defended.

Let's look at ruthlessness again. Spiritual Warriors are utterly ruthless about what they bring into their consciousness. They take the Sword of Truth, cut swiftly and cleanly through all that is extraneous, all the superficialities, the mindsets and addictions that hold them back. This is the Sword of the Heart, the spiritual heart, the heart of our wisdom. As you cut through the waste matter of your life, you may feel resistant and uncomfortable; you may be spacy, sleepy, antsy or distracted. Never fear. Someone once said, "If you don't feel awkward doing something new, you are not doing something new."

Look at a situation that is currently bothering you, and ask yourself these questions:

What situation blocks or challenges me?

What is the illusion in that situation?

What is the truth that I can act upon in that situation?

Close your eyes and use the Sword of Truth, the Sword of the Heart, to cut away the illusion. (If you need to forgive yourself first, do that.) When you feel free of the blocking situation, open your eyes. The idea is to be clear with yourself and to cut away from you that which is dead, and is no longer needed.

Now take a moment to see if there is any qualitative difference inside you and to examine your intention or intent. It is important to realize that this intent is your purpose. It is amazing how many people do not have a purpose in their life. They have some reasons, but they do not have a purpose. I am referring to "purpose" as being that all-consuming thing, like your next breath of air. There is no way you can't take it, no way you can't do it. That is purpose.

Completion

You need to make peace with everyone in your life. Everyone lives inside you. It doesn't matter if they are living or dead, or if you'll never see them again; if they create discord within you, then you have to make peace with them.

Start with the main characters, your parents. For many years I have advocated closure with your parents. Even if your parents are dead, it is not too late to love them and forgive them: And if they are alive, all the better. If you want to complete things with your mother, call her. If that can't be done, take some quiet moments, see her in front of you, and tell her whatever you need to, to bring something incomplete in you to completion. Trust me, she'll get the message. As you talk to her or to others outwardly or inwardly, in this world or in the world of Spirit, you will bring balance and completion to yourself. As you come into reconciliation with yourself, you free up energy that you can use to focus on your intention.

In the world of Spirit there is no time. But you are still here and you are living. Time is precious. This physical world can act as a springboard for you into the higher consciousness. Our bodies, minds, emotions, unconscious, and Soul come together in one place, giving us the best opportunity in the universe for growth and upliftment. So in these last few days of living, use your time for your advancement.

The Spiritual Warrior practices dying every day and experiences rebirth at every minute. This is not physical death, but a willingness to see everything anew in each moment.

It is very important that you understand something: You are here on this planet because you did things incorrectly at some time in your existences. *You did not do it the way it was to be done and you are back here.* And what's more, this may not be the last time if you continue on as you are doing.

That hurt you had years ago—whether it's five or fifteen or fifty years ago—bury it right now. When you are a victim of the past, you are living in the past, and that is death in life. When you were younger, you made decisions and those decisions didn't work and you got hurt. Fine. So you got hurt. But it's over now. Bury it. Let it go and come to the present, because the present is where God resides.

We have been in darkness so long, just so long. If enlightenment comes at the last breath, this life has been totally worthwhile and blessed. If enlightenment does not come at the last breath and never came, you just walked through another living death. You had emotions and you had good feelings and no living love was present. A life with no living love present is not the life of a Spiritual Warrior.

A woman I know went to visit a friend of hers who had only two or three days left to live. She said to the dying woman, "If I had that few days left, I would be up writing things to my children, videotaping, and dictating how I want the housekeeper to take care of the house, and how I want the nursemaid to take care of the kids. And I'd be leaving directions for my husband on how to get another really good wife."

But then, all at once, my friend closed her mouth, and asked herself, "What would I *really* do if I only had three days to live?"

And at that thought she broke down and wept. For the first time the immediacy of death struck her. She realized that the moment of death is not a time to be looking back, to be thinking about the past. That is the time to live in the present.

Death Is Your Friend:
An Exercise for Living Life More Fully

An obituary usually summarizes your life and achievements and the interesting things you did. What if you could write your own obituary with the intention of revealing yourself? After all, you are the only one with the whole, inside story. How do you see your life? We recommend that you do the following exercise. *To gain the greatest value, do it as if you were going to die tomorrow.*

1. Spend a few minutes responding to this question, mentally: *What is the essential message that life has given me?*

2. On a piece of paper, complete this sentence: *If I had known I was going to die so soon....*

3. Now, find a quiet space and a time when you are unlikely to be disturbed, and go ahead and write your obituary. It doesn't need to be more than two pages. Somewhere in the obituary include the sentence you wrote in #2.

4. When you are done, spend 15 minutes in quiet contemplation, forgiving yourself for any judgments you have about any aspect of your life. Spend the last five minutes in gratitude. If you like, you can mentally list all the things you are grateful for.

In the movie *Black Robe*, an Indian chief has a vision of his death. Later on, he comes to the place he saw in his vision. And on his death bed he says if he had known when he had the vision that he was looking at the place of his death, he would have been a greater chief; he would have helped more people, he would have been braver, and so on. In other words, he realizes that since he could not have died before this moment, he could have been more daring, he need not have let his fears hold him back. But by this time it was too late.

How we die is so very important because it will be our last thoughts and our last feelings in this life. How we handle the turmoil of our existence is going to determine our placement in the realms of Spirit when we leave here. So they become very, very important. As a Spiritual Warrior, the life that you have been living up to this point on this planet has been a rehearsal for death. So you have to know how to get away from the body cleanly. You have to know where you are going to place your consciousness. This is why meditation, contemplation, spiritual exercises, prayer—all these things—are very, very important to the spirituality of any individual. The more you dwell upon God and God's love and the extension of that consciousness to you, when it comes to those last moments before you leave, your thoughts will be on that. And to that is where you will go. So it is not a moral or religious statement but a very practical one when I say, yes, keep a clean mind and a clean body and clean emotions by watching where you place them. And if you say, "But, oh, look at all the things I did in the past," so what? You are right: They are past.

Stalking the Spirit

Most of us are afraid of dying. But when we can contact the Spirit inside of us, we find peace, and death seems as natural as breathing. Life presupposes death: Death presupposes life. We play a game with ourselves: We pretend that if we can confuse death, sidetrack death, hide from death, forget about death, death will forget about us. But Spiritual Warriors look death in the face; and this frees them to focus on life. While death is stalking you, you should be stalking Spirit.

If you are a Spiritual Warrior, you can learn through spiritual exercises to leave your body and transcend to the Spirit while still living on this earth. Death then mistakes you as being part of its spiritual beingness and leaves you alone. Not forever, of course, but in the daily dying which is the fear of death. So when you finally die, you die only once, you just die the death of the body.

Sit down in meditation or spiritual exercises and close your eyes; have the intention to stalk the Spirit. The Spirit then starts to love you, and to be loved in you. You move more and more into the Spirit, and a serenity happens in you. It is not a mental thing. It is not what we think of as "happiness." It is an energy field that is, by itself, absolutely whole and complete; it is called God. When we experience this serenity it is as if we touch God. You feel you are the Beloved, then you know you are the Beloved, then you just *are* the Beloved.

The problem is that most people are stalking death. Those who are stalking the Spirit bypass the rules of death's game, slip past the bonds of death into the Light. Death does not deal in love. Neither does it deal with health, wealth, and happiness; prosperity, abundance, and riches; loving, caring, sharing, and touching. It deals with obliterating your consciousness from this level. When we are totally in God, totally free of the fear of death, then at last death leaves us alone. We are no longer running from it and so it cannot recognize us as its prey.

We must be strong in our fearlessness. The moment we slip back, the moment we start thinking, "Oh my God, maybe I'll die. Maybe I'll fall. Maybe I'll . . . " Death says, "Oh, there you are; I thought I lost you," and starts to stalk you again. This we must not allow. Through prayer, meditation, contemplation, spiritual exercises, service, and love we conquer death.

The Spiritual Warrior looks at death and loves death. Death comes not as one who obliterates, but as one who releases from pain and sorrow.

The people who have learned to see death as a release from the pain of this earth welcome it as a real friend. Death is transformed from the grim reaper to the giver of new opportunity. Stalk the Spirit. Spiritual Warriors stalk the spirit of life.

The Heart: An Exercise in Loving Yourself

Try reading the following into a tape recorder. Then play it back and *observe*, hearing not yourself, but the Spirit speaking to you.

It is the Spirit that speaks the words to your heart. Listen to that heart, and fill it up with Divinity.

Breathe it, feel the heart expanding, and feel the energy in your heart.

Take a few moments to touch this heart area. You can put both your hands over it and just know that the Divinity and the loving exist. Just know that, and feel it.

If you get goose bumps or you sharply inhale or you experience energy moving, that is an indication that you are starting to move into it. Stay present with it; don't move your mind to something else. Only do this. Stay with this.

Placing your hands over the heart keeps you kinesthetically tied to it.

Tell yourself, "This is love. This one is love. . ."

Now if someplace in your body does not feel well, just have that love extend over and touch it. If you start to move away from it, bring it back. Touch it again and feel it. Say, "This is Divinity. This is love. This is where it is inside of me. From my heart and my heart center I give love to all of my body."

If you feel a funny sensation in your stomach, reach down and touch it.

If you are starting to feel something on the top of your head, touch it.

Say, "This love arcs to that or goes through me to that."

If you are not having success, think of something that you really love, like your spouse, your child, your life, God. Take that feeling and make it come awake in your heart, because it is your Divinity. It is yours. When that hits, flood your body with it and you will find yourself being a commutator of Divine energy and it will be flooding down all around you.

Love is the healer. Joy is the expression.

The Value of Life

As has been discussed, death can be looked upon as a release. We can use this concept in our daily lives. It has been called dying each day. Look at what presently bothers you or what you are obsessed with. What if you died tomorrow? How important would those things be to you? From that perspective, usually not very important at all. The fact is, there is really nothing important going on in our lives. We give things importance. We energize them. We build monuments to them. And then we say they must be important, because look at all the energy I spent on them. But it will serve you to understand that the only thing important is the Soul because that is eternal; everything else is in a state of decay.

An Exercise in Observing Life on Earth

Set aside a day that you can devote *entirely to yourself*. At the start of the day, imagine that you have just died. What responsibilities remain to you? None. There is nothing you need to accomplish, nowhere you need to be. All you are going to do is assume you are dead, and observe the world and its people from this perspective. You won't be doing much talking, for you no longer have a voice; and you'll find there is nothing to say. You are just going to be with you, your Soul and its energy. Without distraction, without interruption, you will hold your intention with ease—no effort, no tension, just Spirit. You can take some simple food, but don't let it distract you or rob you of energy. For this one day, time is not important, for there is no time in Spirit. The only time is now.

You can become aware that there are more things going on in life than you could possibly have participated in when you were alive. Also, you did not know where you had come from before you were alive, so you did not know that you had already done the things you did in that last life many times before, and you were stuck in them. All your worries and concerns and self-importance had failed to advance you to the next level of expression.

In fact, you observe that you were back on the same

level of expression and perhaps even expressing the same way. So when we think we are so tuned in about our past lives, what is so great about that? No wonder it seems so familiar.

So in this exercise, just think to yourself: What could I do differently to advance to that next level? What is going to do it? Think about whether, if you could have a special gift or blessing, you could do better? Could you walk through that place called Earth and stay free, keeping your heart and your focus on your intention? The idea is, if you could be granted a wish, a blessing, or a gift you could bring back with you that could assist you, what would it be? Your immediate thought may be more money. But as you may have noticed, not everyone who has money to spare is deliriously happy. It is the internal qualities that count. So give this some serious attention.

For now, sit back and relax, because the next chapter will give you a series of instructions for living life on Earth on your day of observation. Be sure to re-read it on the morning of the day you do the exercise that has just been described.

Chapter 10

Observing Life on Earth: Tips for Travelers

The only thing you can do on the planet

is the best you can.

The people on the Earth do it the best they can,

and then they say it wasn't the best they could.

And then they worry about that,

because they could have done better.

And if they are given another chance

they will do it the same way the second time too.

And a third, and a fourth, and fifth, and sixth.

What you might say to them is,

"If you could have done better,

you would have done better,

and you did the best you could."

John-Roger

The following is a transcript of a lecture I gave to a group of students preparing to do an exercise as if they were visiting the planet Earth. I now share it with the Spiritual Warriors.

One way to experience life on planet Earth is in a scientific framework, as a spiritual scientist. I am not talking about the science that teaches, "Decide what you want to find and then go find it." I am talking about the science of seeing what is there and then recording it and letting it tell you what is present all the time, so that you are always the student, always the one learning. This exercise will serve as a reminder that the Spiritual Warrior observes first, and then strives to be understanding and accepting—always.

As soon as you stop observing and try to tell someone what is there, you start to become the teacher. Don't be. You are a tourist. You are supposed to be observing the humans, not wearing the cloak of guru. If you are not careful, you will have your visas revoked.

Be careful of the trap when humans start saying, "Teach me." If you were to ask them, "Can you learn?" they will say, "Yes," because humans will say just about anything. Especially if it is a man looking at a woman or vice-versa. They will promise each other everything and give each other just about nothing.

So when somebody says, "It's this," you look at it. Then you walk around and you look at it again. And you walk around the other way and look at it again. Then you walk on the other side and look, and then look underneath it. You look at it in every way possible. When you have finished looking, don't tell them what you have found, because if you do they are going to call you a fanatic or a radical in order to try and stop you.

At best, all you can do is suggest to them that they might want to look at things from a broader perspective. That is the viewing point. Don't be attached to the outcome of what you look at, because you didn't put it there. All you are doing is recording what is there. That is the scientific method, and we can use that scientific method to look at their life.

We need the viewing point because if you rely on what they tell you, you are going to have a problem; they lie a lot. And they will fabricate stories and they will mislead you, and they will speak in innuendoes. And then they will say, "I didn't do it." And when you catch them in the act, they will say, "It wasn't my fault, somebody else made me do it. I was brainwashed."

❧ ❧ ❧

They will talk, but the thing they need most is what you are going to supply, which is a loving awareness that the God they worship lives inside them. You see, while they were being implanted with their own Divine nature they were also set up in a game. The game was called, "It's out there, keep going until you find it." They call it, "Searching for success."

However, once they turn inward and find it there, then the people who are teaching the outward approach are going to be out of a job, and they are going to try to crucify you. And you have to be careful that they don't.

You don't have to guard yourself, you just have to watch your mouth. Because your mouth will get you in trouble, like their mouths get them in trouble.

✿   ✿   ✿

People on Earth like to worry a lot. Above all, they like to be right. They are going to tell you they are right. Then they are going to wonder if they are. You see, some of the books they have say one thing, and there are others that say the opposite. And they are both accurate.

So be sure that you don't pick up too many books and carry them around with you because they are going to make you think that you are intelligent. You won't be, because if you are smart you wouldn't be carrying around those books. You would let someone else carry around the books, because there's not too much in them that you are going to find truly valuable.

✿   ✿   ✿

Earth people are going to call you names to upset you. They are going to call you names like, "dumb," "stupid," and "idiot." You have an IQ higher than the names they are calling you, so it is quite obvious they don't know what they are talking about. But please, don't laugh at them. Because then they will get annoyed and get somebody else to call you names too. And because two of them are doing it, they will both agree that they must be right. That's okay. You treat that abuse the way that a bucket of water treats you when you've stuck your hand in it and pulled your hand out again; it retains no impression from you. That is how you treat them.

So don't bother yourself about it. You just listen to what they have to say and be polite, and acknowledge their point of view. You don't have to believe what they say because they have a strange commodity called "emotions." Now, on your day off, you tourists on Earth won't be dealing with a lot of emotions. But to humans, these emotions—wow!—they will die for their emotions. We all know that they are going to die anyway. But they are willing to die early if someone challenges their emotions.

What stimulates their emotions? Their emotions are often involved with things they want to possess. For example, they want to possess the dirt they stand on: "That's my dirt." They are going to want to possess the backyard: "I have a fence around it, get out!" And they will have a piece of paper that has a little, funny seal on the stamp which is recorded someplace else that says it is their land. And everyone who comes to read it will fall down and worship and say, "That's so!" Because that is the way it is done. Now this may sound ridiculous, but if you get in their yard and you are not supposed to be there, they can shoot you. And that will hurt. They may not kill you. But they will yell at you and shout, "I'll kill you!" And sometimes that hurts worse than if they were to shoot you.

But if they do shoot you, being funny creatures they will feel bad afterwards, because they have a thing called "guilt."

Now we know guilt doesn't do anything for you, but they think it does. So they will do things

**that aren't right, and then feel guilty—and then
that lets them do it again.**

Then they feel guilty, and it hurts so badly they punish
themselves. Now, you people all know that when you
want to be punished you just smack yourself and it's
over with.

Not these people on Earth. They don't do that. They
think about it, and think about it, and feel bad about it,
and feel worse about it, and moan and groan and complain of how guilty they feel. Then if you ask them, "How
many times have you done that?" they will answer, "Lots
of times." It will be time for you to move on to somewhere else because it is obvious they are not going to
learn anything.

❧   ❧   ❧

Remember, the planet Earth is set up as a big board
game. Whatever you do, you have to make the best of
everything. Now, in reality, there is not going to be anything bad happening, but they are going to talk about
disasters, and catastrophes, and crises, and emergen-
cies. And the amazing thing is, the Earth people have
all had hundreds of them. Yes, each one
has had at least a hundred crises and catastrophes. But
don't ask about the crises, because that just keeps
reminding them, and they will run them down for you
immediately: "This happened, that, this, and this,
and this, and this, and this!" They love to talk about
them.

But if you ask them about anything good that has happened, it will take them quite awhile to think about that. You see, they are not aware that they got through the catastrophes and the disasters pretty well.

❧   ❧   ❧

These Earth people have alibis, and excuses, and reasons for everything. Whatever they have, they will have a reason for it. They can spend all day long on a street corner talking to people, and they will stand there all night long talking. And all the next day they are still talking. They will just smoke and drink and then, when they run out of money, they go and they take it from somebody else. They go up to them and say, "Give me your money." And the other person says, "You'll have to kill me first." So they do.

The person who said "You'll have to kill me first," apparently forgot that they had more money at home, and they could have reached in their pocket and said, "Oh, here's the money, bye." But, no, they are going to die for it. What they do is take that money and just spend it on worthless stuff. They don't know where it is half the time and then they throw it away later on.

Their value system is backwards. They value the material things that are going to disappear. The spiritual things, they don't even know about. They say they do, but they say a lot of things. So whatever you do, don't believe what they say. That doesn't mean that some of them aren't going to tell you the truth. They keep you off guard.

❀   ❀   ❀

Earth people will say, "You never pay any attention to me." The other person will say, "Yes, I do." And they will say, "No, you don't." And the other person will say, "Well, if I'm not paying attention to you, how could I argue back with you now?" And they will say, "You always argue about the wrong things." You see, they always have an answer for everything.

❀   ❀   ❀

When you go to planet Earth, all you have to do is play the game. But don't get caught up in it. Don't start defending your car. Don't start defending anything because somebody is going to come along and hit it or take it. You can say, "I guess if you're going to use it, you're going to use it."

❀   ❀   ❀

And some of them are going to dress their bodies up in the most awful looking things, and go out and walk up and down the street to show how pretty they are. They are pretty without all those things, but they don't believe it. So they will paint themselves also. Not all of them, but some of them. And they are going to do all sorts of strange things to their bodies to look more beautiful. But we all know that they were made in God's image, which means they are already the most beautiful. But they forgot to look where the beauty is. They just look on the surface of the body and out in the world.

Some of them have found that if they look into a person's eyes and relax, and the other person relaxes, they see something in there very dynamic and beautiful. But it scares them. They say, "I don't want to look in there! I'm scared. I thought I saw God. Or a bright light. Oh, that frightens me. Don't tell me that's inside of me. If God was in me, I would know it wouldn't I? Well, wouldn't I? Of course! Anybody would know if God's in there. They would know it because it would explode you." See how they can reason that? And they are not exploded so they will tell you there is no God, and they have their proof.

When they show you the proof, just say, "Yeah, that's pretty good proof." That's all. They will think you are saying, "That's the best proof there is." And then they will go down the street saying that you said, "This is the best proof there is." There is no need to deny it, because next they are going to call you a liar and a hypocrite and all sorts of other names, but they will still use you as proof anyway. So you are going to be a lying hypocrite and used as an authority to prove something for them. I don't know how you are going to play that role very well, but they are going to demand that you do it.

❉   ❉   ❉

The only thing you can do on the planet is the best you can. The people on the Earth do it the best they can, and then they say it wasn't the best they could. And then they worry about that, because they could have done better. And if they are given another chance they will do it the same way the second time too. And a third, and a fourth, and fifth, and sixth. What you might say to them is, "If you could have done better, you would have done better, and you did the best you could." And then when they say, "Prove it," say, "Look at what you did." You will see them be astounded by the miracle of your perception because they never take time to look at that.

❉   ❉   ❉

If you get involved with one of them in an intimate way, they are going to want you to change what you are doing. They are going to love you for what you are now, and when you get close with them, they are going to make you change all of that. The things that you do that they like, after being close, they will try to get you to stop doing them. And the reason they wanted to be with you in the first place was for that "cute" thing you do! But after you stop doing it, they are not going to love you any more and they are not going to want to be with you. And if you go to do it again, that is going to prove you don't love them, and they are going to want to separate anyway. So you can see why those people get divorced a lot. An awful lot.

Observing Life on Earth: Tips for Travelers

❀   ❀   ❀

They are not too sure what to do with their kids yet. They keep trying to give them away. But they will fight for them, because that is the thing to do, because everybody says, "Oh, look how good they are." But then, when they get them, they aren't sure they want them, because later on, the kids say strange things like, "Give us the car, give us the money, we deserve it, we're your kids. Give us a bicycle."

And if they catch one of their kids doing something wrong, the kid will stand there saying, "I did not! I did not! I did not!" He will stand there for hours, and hours until the parents get tired and walk away. Then the kid says, "All I've got to do is wear them down. They're getting old, I've just got to outlast them." And every day that the mother and father get older, the kid gets stronger. But after all, he has learned how to do that because of the way they taught him.

So watch how kids are being taught, because they are the next generation. You can tell what is going to happen on the planet by seeing what the children are being taught. There is some hope, but not a lot. If only they could really practice what they preach; to honestly love each other, and not judge. The irony is that every one of them down on that planet has been taught, "Don't judge." And they will swear, "Dear God, I won't judge." Then they will judge up a storm! They do the worst judgments you can think of, and if there is nothing real to judge, they will make it up. Then when somebody catches them in a lie, they say, "Well, it looked like that to me. And that's my opinion and I can have my own opinion." So everyone has a right to their own opinion, right or wrong. When you say, "But you're saying things that aren't right," they say, "The First Amendment says I can do that."

So, I think you realize that the Earth was really put there as a crazy house, and all the people down there are crazy! They keep talking about not going to hell, not realizing that by talking about it and focusing on it, they are in hell! And each one goes around with their own little God, saying they have the real God. And they say, "Give up yours, and come and look at mine." So feel free to go over and take a look, because you will see a lot of strange looking ones. Some of them will say that they are God, clear down to their toes. But we all know that God is inside of them and resides even outside the toes. But they don't know that.

You see, they think their body is God. They worship how their body looks. Then when it dies, they take it and they do all sorts of lavish, expensive things that they never did for it when it was alive! And they go up to the bodies lying there and say, "Oh, God! I really shouldn't have done that to you, I should have told you how much I loved you. I really did, and I shouldn't have done those terrible things. Oh, God forgive me!" But they won't tell them that while

they are alive. They send them flowers when they are dead, and they can't smell them.

They have a saying down there, "Repent." That means stop the bad things you are doing, and then you find God. They call it the Kingdom of God. A lot of them are saying, "Show me the Kingdom of God first, and then I'll see if it's worth repenting." Because maybe what they are doing is better than what they will get. So they bargain with God all the time. "Oh, God! Get me out of this, and I'll never do it again." Then when they get it they say, "It's okay God, you don't have to, I got out by myself, and the deal's off." They don't know that God is listening and helping anyway.

Some of them are wising up. Those are the people who are spiritual. You won't be able to tell who they are from any of the others, because they will look the same. But if you look into their eyes, you will see them there looking back at you. And they say, "Hi!" and they get this mischievous look and you think, "What are you doing in there?" Be careful, because they might tell you, "I'm waiting for you!"

Some of them have a tremendous amount of fun. In fact, you can tell the spiritual ones; they have a lot of joy and humor inside them and they know that some things can be called "serious" even when they are not, and they pretend. Of course, as soon as that's over, they have a lot of fun again.

But all in all, I think you get the idea: It can be very fun down with these people on Earth. If you have a good sense of humor, don't lose it. Because there are a lot of places where you can lose it. They lose it with people called "husbands, and wives, and children, and bosses." So if somebody brings one of those words to you, chuckle every time you hear it.

They will tell you, "They caused me heartache. I said I would give them my heart. I told them how much I loved them and they gave me heartache. So with the next one I'm just going to *say* I'll give them my heart, but I won't give it. So I'm going to lie to them first thing out, and then I'm going to live with them the rest of the time.

When I get to the end of the relationship, I'll say, 'I didn't mean it, please forgive me.'" Do you know what? The other person will. They are the most forgiving bunch of people, but they don't forget. You know that true forgiveness is when you forget it. So when you're there and somebody comes up to you and says, "Forgive me," just say, "Forget it."

If you are able to maintain your objectivity by truly observing life on Earth, you will do fine. But remember, if you start getting involved in the things I have described, you will most likely forget what I have told you.

Enjoy your visit to Earth.

PART III

Maintaining Spiritual Convergence

A Fifteen Day Journal

Here is an exercise that will give you more practical experience in the work of the Spiritual Warrior.

Start a journal for the next fifteen days. For each day, write your prime intention for that day at the top of a new page in your journal. Start each day by reading the designated passage. Each passage will provide a focus for your awareness as you move along your intention. At the end of that day read the same passage again and then write a paragraph or two about your experience. This exercise will assist you in converging your spirit back into alignment.

DAY ONE

You come into this world attempting to fulfill certain qualities within yourself, and you go about it in many ways. But everyone has a prime directive: *You are here to find out who you are, to find out where your home in Spirit is, to go there in consciousness, and to have co-creative consciousness with God, the Supreme Father.* This is our whole direction and purpose on this planet. This is where your satisfaction and your fulfillment lie.

DAY TWO

It is quite obvious that the Spirit does not care if it is fair or not fair. Spirit is ruthless. Not the kind of ruthlessness that hits you on the head or cuts your arm off and lets you bleed to death, but ruthless in the sense that if your intention is not oriented toward it, it does not reveal itself to you. And if, after all the trials, tribulations, and troubles that we have gone through to reach it, it doesn't say "hello" or do anything, it seems like a gross unfairness.

Here is the paradox: Spirit has always been there. And for the most part, we have always been there. If we have been there, and It has been there, why are we not knowing that we are both there? What is this thing inside of us that stops us from knowing what is going on?

DAY THREE

When we were born in this world, we sacrificed a spiritual world. When we were born here we entered into a condition called sacrifice. In the spiritual world where we existed as Spirit, as pure love, we looked down into this material world, and from that high plane of love, we saw where we could do everything perfectly. But in the place we were looking from, everything looked perfect. So then we decided to go into this place called Earth. We all know what happens when you get here. It does not go the way you want it to. So, therefore, we say it is not perfect. But, as a matter of scientific truth, everything here is perfect. We just don't like it the way it is. So the problem is not what is here. The problem is our attitude toward it.

DAY FOUR

We don't belong here spiritually. We are engrafted into the body. That is why we have such a hard time making ourselves do what we want to do according to our intention, because our intention only functions in the Spirit.

DAY FIVE

You are not here just to do what you know how to do.
You are not here just to learn what you already know.
You are here to learn what you do not know and what
you do not know how to do. You are going to do it, and
it is not necessarily easy or hard. It is just a matter of
doing it. In doing it, willpower becomes "willingness,"
willingness becomes "ability," ability becomes "openness," and when convergence takes place it is "grace."
Then, we come into alignment once again.

DAY SIX

There is a law: If something can be shaken, it will be shaken. But that shaking will be done by you and your thoughts and your feelings. You will shake yourself harder than anyone else can shake you. That is why your mind is your enemy because it will go against you in your Spirit. And it seems to win because although your Spirit, the Soul, is the Spiritual Warrior, the mind is the physical armored warrior who will attempt to destroy and wreak havoc and vengeance and set loose the dogs of war on your neighbor, or your spouse, or your kids, or even yourself.

People will try to antagonize you, baiting you to strike at them. But the Spiritual Warrior withholds the strike, knowing full well that the karma they set in motion will be worse than any blow. The Spiritual Warrior looks at his antagonist and says, "Get behind me. If I strike, I fall."

DAY SEVEN

The prime way to build your endurance as a Spiritual Warrior is through the inner work of meditation, contemplation, prayer, and spiritual exercises. I recommend spiritual exercises as the most direct approach because once the connection is made into the Soul energy, the armor of God becomes your armor.

But the way endurance is built in the world—whether we like it or not—is through adversity. We are strengthened through adversity, and how we handle the adversity is the critical measure of our growth. Anyone can stand and argue and yell back; anyone can call somebody names. But when you call me a name and I absorb it and gain strength from it, you have lost me as an adversary.

DAY EIGHT

Life has this message for all those who, in their self-importance, want to help others: Don't get involved in things that are not your immediate level of concern. Don't take on someone else's concerns. If you take on someone's karma and you start to carry it, guess what the person who originally had the karma has to do? They still have to carry it. So now there are two of you. And what if their burden is to carry a big backpack full of rocks up and down a hill? That is what you start to do. And if you wonder why you have backaches and headaches and leg aches, it is because you are in something that is not yours. Get out of it.

You may say, "I can't let go. This is a friend." No, this is not a friend. This is a karmic burden that is theirs. You delay them by your supposed idea of friendship. There is a form of ruthlessness that must come into friendship—where you draw some boundary lines with each other. And you make sure that these lines are not crossed. This is really caring in the greatest way. Because if you take karma away from someone, and you take it away too soon, you may be damning them to suffering all over again through the same pattern.

DAY NINE

In living life as a Spiritual Warrior, there are going to be times when you are forced by your situation and circumstances to look more deeply at who you are and what you are about. Take some time to look within yourself, see who is in there, and become one with it.

When you have found the true *you* and you are really living that life, you will find that you don't care whether you live or die, because that part of you will always exist. When you are there, dying becomes a grace. I have seen people get to that point just a day or two before death. And I have seen some get to it on their next-to-last breath.

It doesn't matter when you reach that state. What matters is simply that you reach it. So, do it now because the Spiritual Warrior lives from the inside out.

DAY TEN

Being critical is not impeccability. Using things against yourself or others is a waste of energy. But you can take your critical nature and use it to perfect yourself. This way you can be your own petty tyrant. Stop fearing poverty. Find the wealth from the Spirit inside of you. Do not parade your emotions as compassion when they also bring hurt to you. Do not place value on things in the world, but place value on the things in your Spirit. From out of your Spirit move into the world and let your Spirit direct your motion. Do not let your thoughts, feelings, or ego move you; let your heart move you. It will move you with its wisdom and knowledge. Sometimes it will tell you a little bit ahead of time, or it may just walk you into it and see how you handle it. But with Spirit with you, you won't be given what cannot be handled. You will see each challenge as an opportunity to test and develop your talents impeccably.

DAY ELEVEN

Keep ever watchful. When you are truly alive and joyfully awake, negative power cannot trap you. To trap you, it has to find a pattern of negativity in which you are involved, run it out in a time pattern, and lay a trap for you to fall into. But if you are in the moment, loving right now, blissfully awake and alert, and you come up to a trap, you will see it, sidestep it, and keep on going.

DAY TWELVE

You acknowledge Spirit's presence by allowing It into your life without restriction or conditions. Spirit does not care how, where, or when It touches you, because It is not a respecter of persons and It does not care what you think about It. Whether you want the healing now, last week, or in a month, It moves on Its own and in Its own time. And your job as a Spiritual Warrior is to be ready to receive of the Spirit at any time and at all times.

DAY THIRTEEN

If God is truly present in the now (and believe me, He is), what concern do you have for the past or the future? What do you care if you live or die? You may feel fear. You may say, "but I don't want to die, not now, not ever."

But you are not dying right now. Why are you fighting what does not exist now, what is not happening now? If you are going to die now, you are going to die now, whether or not you are worrying about it. And if you are not going to die now, you are not going to die now, whether or not you are worrying about it. Worrying, to me, is a very hard way to die.

DAY FOURTEEN

A great deal of the stress that people suffer is a result of not living right now, of being totally occupied with the past or the future. This is the cause of so many troubles. When you cut out your concern for the future and your remembrance of the past, you are right here, now. Many people try to remember to be here now. However, when they try to remember, the very act of remembering throws them out of the now. If you stop remembering, or you forget to remember, and just be here now, you are in good territory. Hold yourself in the now.

DAY FIFTEEN

When you go to see the Soul, you mostly see your thoughts and nothing else. So you say, "There's nothing else. If there were, I would be able to see it." You can't see the Soul's existence because it is wrapped up in you. Your Soul is what keeps you alive, not your mind. The mind, as strong as it may sometimes seem, is not always to be trusted. The Soul is solid ground.

Models of the Spiritual Warrior
(An Invitation)

It has been said that there are no heroes these days. Everyone that reaches prominence seems to have an Achilles heel at best and feet of clay at worst. The same might be said of Spiritual Warriors; there are none today. But that would be incorrect because no one said Spiritual Warriors had to be perfect.

In future editions of this book, I would like to include a list of people, real or fictional, who represent the characteristics of the Spiritual Warrior to you. As an exercise, make a list of the people who personify for you a quality or qualities identified as those of the Spiritual Warrior. Qualities like:

>Intention
>Impeccability
>Ruthlessness
>Dedication
>Commitment
>Discipline

Focus
Acceptance
Cooperation
Understanding
Enthusiasm
Empathy
Surrender
Health, Wealth, Happiness
Prosperity, Abundance, Riches
Loving, Caring, Sharing, and Touching

Name the person, and describe what characteristic(s) of the Spiritual Warrior they demonstrate. Be as creative and as open as the Spiritual Warrior in you allows.

Send your list to Mandeville Press, P.O. Box 513935, Los Angeles, CA 90051-1935, Attn: Spiritual Warrior, or send e-mail to **jrbooks@msia.org**.

Afterword

Here is the paradox:
Spirit has always been there.
And for the most part,
we have always been there.
If we have been there,
and It has been there,
why are we not knowing that we are both there?

Additional Support and Study Materials

Since 1963, John-Roger has been lecturing and teaching about practical spirituality; how to use universal spiritual principles to create happiness, health, wealth and a life filled with loving.

From among his vast body of work, we have selected the following materials for those who are interested in learning more about the ideas presented in *Spiritual Warrior.*

Books by John Roger

Forgiveness: The Key to the Kingdom
What is the one thing that, if we all did it, would revolutionize our lives? What is the single most important element in getting a "fresh start?" What do we want from others and need even from ourselves? Forgiveness. God's business is forgiveness and we can make it our most important business, too. This easy-to-read book is full of personal stories and anecdotes that turn us inward to our own hearts and lead us into God's heart.
ISBN 0-914829-34-3
$12.50 softcover

Additional Support and Study Materials

Inner Worlds Of Meditation
Practicing the various forms of meditation can produce results ranging from stress reduction to higher states of awareness. Often looked upon as a passive and sometimes boring pursuit, meditation is presented here as the vital, active, and exciting process it can be.
ISBN 0-914829-45-9
$12.00 softcover

The Power Within You
The tools for creating what you want are within your reach; your greatest tools and resources lie within. Discover the powerful, positive use of your conscious, subconscious, and unconscious mind. Practice and develop the skill of working with your inner success mechanism. Readers will find that this book expands their personal power—an invaluable tool for those who want to build a better world in and around them.
ISBN 0-914829-24-6
$10.00 softcover

The Tao of Spirit
This beautifully designed collection of writings was inspired by the Tao Te Ching, a book written by the venerable Chinese sage Lao-Tzu in the sixth century B.C.. Designed to help you let go of the stress of daily living and turn to the stillness within, the chapters have been organized so that they can be read as a daily or weekly inspiration. What a wonderful way to start or to end the day—remembering to let go of your day-to-day problems and frustrations and be refreshed in the source at the center of your existence. Incorporating quotes from William Blake, Wordsworth, Shakespeare, Whitman, Rumi, and others, it is a book to live by.
ISBN 0-914829-33-5
$15.00 hardcover

John-Roger

Walking With the Lord
For anyone interested in spiritual exercises, or for anyone who wants a deeper relationship with God, this guide is indispensable. It is a handbook that provides instruction in meditation, in chanting the name of God, and in dealing with mental and emotional distractions that tend to get in the way.
ISBN 0-914829-30-0
$12.50 softcover

Resource Materials

The following resource materials are available through the Movement of Spiritual Inner Awareness, 213/737-4055, P.O. Box 513935, Los Angeles, CA 90051-1935.

Spiritual Warrior Audio Tape Packet
This is a set of three audio tapes, each building and strengthening a different aspect of the Spiritual Warrior. This is a valuable resource to assist you in aligning with the Spiritual Warrior in your daily life.

The packet includes:

1. *Innerphasing to the Precious Presence*
An innerphasing tape is used every day for 33 days, so the power of the content's intention steadily builds and creates a solid foundation within you. The focus of this innerphasing tape is learning to live in the now.

2. *Dying Each Day*
We know loving ourself unconditionally is desirable, but often difficult to achieve. This audio tape provides keys and a meditation for doing just that. It supports you in loving all aspects of your self and contains an exercise for putting Light on all levels of your consciousness.

3. *Convergent Moment*
This is a great tape to play during meditation or spiritual exercises. It contains a series of excerpts of John-Roger speaking about different aspects of the Spiritual Warrior, separated by periods of silence for meditation or contemplation. This is an outstanding resource for enhancing spiritual exercises.
#3905, $25

Spiritual Warrior
This tape, available in audio or video format, stands among those which provide a foundation for practicing Spiritual Warriorhood. In clear English, with simultaneous Spanish language translation, John-Roger defines the job of the Spiritual Warrior, and what must be done to bring forward the Sword of Truth inside your heart.
#7333, $10   #V-7333, $20

Soul Awareness Discourses—A Home Study Course for Your Spiritual Growth
The heart of John-Roger's teachings, Soul Awareness Discourses provide a structured and methodical approach to gaining greater awareness of ourselves and our relationship to the world and to God. Each year's study course contains twelve lessons, one for each month. Discourses offer a wealth of practical keys to more successful living. Even more, they provide keys to the greater spiritual knowledge and awareness of the Soul.
$100 one-year subscription

John-Roger

Soul Awareness Tape Club Series
This tape-a-month club provides members with a new John-Roger talk every month on a variety of topics ranging from practical living to spiritual upliftment. In addition, members of the SAT Club may purchase previous SAT releases, several of which are included in the resource materials listed below.
$100 one-year subscription

Audio and Video Tapes by John-Roger

Tapes indicated by an asterisk (*) are available only to SAT Club members. Videotapes are indicated by a V in the order number. If you would like a catalog listing all of John-Roger's audio and videotapes and books, please write or call to request one.

Are You Experiencing Your Prosperity? #3411
Are Your Protecting Your Weakness? #3214
Authentic Empowerment #7426 & #V-7426
Awareness is Power #2135
By Way of Karma or Grace #3412
Faith Extension vs. Phony Front* #7445
God is Intention #7354 & #V-7354
How Are You Measuring Up? #7450 & #V-7450
How Do You Con Yourself? #7406 & #V-7406
Knowing Your God Essence #7391
Living in a Positive Attitude #2137
Manifesting God's Abundance #1477
On Death and Dying* #1381
Psychic Violence #7308 & #V-7308
Psychic-Sexual Energies #3208
Relationships: Rescuing You or Saving Me?* #7044
The Convergence with Spirit #7340 & #V-7340

Additional Support and Study Materials

The Known, The Unknown and the Unknowable* #7361
The Suffering of Man, His Dilemma and The White Light
    Meditation #2591
Thou Shalt Not Have Other Gods Before Me* #7394
Travelers on the Nile #7211
Ways and Means of Spiritual Convergence* #7363
What Converges the Spirit? #7337 & #V-7337
What is the Greatest Courage? #1309
What's Your Percentage? #7403 & #V-7403
Who Has Ownership Over Your Life? #7255 & #V-7255
Who Is Your Life Based On? #2637

Audio Tapes, $10
SAT Audio Tapes, $9
Video Tapes, $20

About the Author

A teacher and lecturer of international stature, with millions of books in print, John-Roger is a luminary in the lives of thousands of people. For over three decades, his wisdom, humor, common sense and love have helped people to discover the Spirit within themselves and find health, peace, and prosperity.

With two co-authored books on the *New York Times* Best-seller List to his credit, and more than three dozen spiritual and self-help books and audio albums, John-Roger is an extraordinary resource for a wide range of subjects. He is the founder of the nondenominational Church of the Movement of Spiritual Inner Awareness (MSIA), which focuses on Soul Transcendence; President of the Institute for Individual and World Peace; Chancellor of the University of Santa Monica; and President of Peace Theological Seminary and College of Philosophy.

John-Roger has given over 5,000 seminars worldwide, many of which are televised nationally on his cable program, "That Which Is." He has been a featured guest on CNN's "Larry King Live" and appears regularly on radio and television.

An educator and minister by profession, John-Roger continues to transform the lives of many, by educating them in the wisdom of the spiritual heart.

If you've enjoyed this book, you may want to explore and delve more deeply into what John-Roger has shared about this and other related topics. For more information on John-Roger's teachings through the Movement of Spiritual Inner Awareness, please contact:

MSIA®
P.O. Box 513935
Los Angeles, CA 90051-1935
213/737-4055
soul@msia.org
www.msia.org

Acknowledgments

As anyone who has written a book knows, it takes a collaborative effort of many people. My special thanks go to Paul Kaye for taking my lectures and skillfully recognizing the book within them. To Laren Bright for putting the words into a form that people could read. To Paul Cohen for believing in the project from the start. To Simon Warwick-Smith and Associates for telling everyone. To Sally Kirkland and Leigh Taylor-Young for putting themselves out there, always. To Van Hill and Associated Publishers Group for making all the right moves, at all the right times, in all the right directions. To Judi Goldfader for her know-how, know-who, no-matter-what, joyful approach. And to John Morton who is one of my heroes and role models for the *Spiritual Warrior*. Thank you.